NC

BOMBER COMMAND

The Story of Francis Norman Crouch

The first Australian to fly a Lancaster Bomber in WWII

1.8.1920 – 8.7.2003

JAMES CROUCH

Copyright Notice

 Published by Footprints Publishing, August 2020

© All rights reserved by the author.

 A catalogue record for this work is available from the National Library of Australia

ISBN (sc): 978-0-6487145-2-1

ISBN (hc): 978-0-6487145-3-8

ISBN (e): 978-0-6487145-7-6

Margery aged 92 and dressed up in her pearls and brooch. 2012

1982 reunion in Toronto, Canada with his 2 gunners. Norm in middle, Jack Oates the rear gunner on his right and Bill Townley the mid-upper gunner on his left.

DEDICATIONS

For my mother and father.

PREFACE

As a boy, my father was my hero. He flew aeroplanes. He was an airline captain with Trans Australia Airways (TAA) and his uniform had gold bands on its tunic's sleeves. But there was something more that was not obvious to a child. It was the way he was spoken to by those who knew him. His family and a few friends had a respect for him that seemed different and the source intangible.

Dad was a quiet man who rarely spoke of his war experiences and it was only when he got together with his brother Stuart that the veil was lifted, and the conversation would sometimes turn to Bomber Command. Both my father and uncle had completed a tour there and survived. They had survived the deadliest theatre of World War II. When I started compiling the information for Norm's story the statistics were astounding:

125,000 Aircrew served in RAF Bomber Command, 57,861 never returned home.

*Lincolnshire Aviation Heritage Centre.

One in five combat deaths of Australians in the war were in Bomber Command.

*The Hon Dr Brendan Nelson,
Bomber Command Commemorative Address 2017.

It was the air force that incurred the highest casualty rate of all Allied Forces in WWII. There were 6500 RAAF airmen who lost their lives in combat. Fully 83 per cent of these men (5400) were killed in the European theatre alone. Of those who died in Europe, two-thirds (3486) died while serving with Bomber Command.

* Air Power Development Centre. Department of Defence

June 2012

In Norm's case, of those Australians who left in early 1941 and completed a full tour, 30 missions or more and then spent the rest of the war flying and training others in Operational Training Command, only 8% returned.

Norm knew he had a story to tell and when our house burned down in 1957 he lost all his records from the war including his personal logbook. He then wrote his memories so his story would not be lost and I have used them along with other sources which I acknowledge later.

CONTENTS

The Early Years   1

Learning to Fly   6

The RAAF   9

Coventried   13

The Empire Air Training Scheme   16

Flying Training in Canada and Running Grog   20

The Convoy   24

England   27

Operations Against the Enemy   32

The Lancaster   45

Low Flying and the Augsberg Raid   49

The Tirpitz   53

The First 1,000 Bomber Raid – Cologne 'Coventried'   56

Taking Over As Skipper   58

Gardening – Minelaying   62

Kassel   64

Brighton Disciplinary Unit   69

Last Mission   71

92 Group – Training Command   73

Margery   78

Dam Busters   81

Stuart Crouch   83

Clark Gable   89

Kettleby Thorpe Farm   94

Return to an Ungrateful Country   109

Civil Flying Career   111

Retirement   120

Epilogue   123

Bibliography

Acknowledgments

THE EARLY YEARS

The year was 1935 when Norm saw his first aeroplane. He was 15 years old and riding his bike near his home in the Sydney suburb of Pymble, which was then an affluent outer suburb north of Sydney with large properties branching out into the gently undulating countryside. There was a lot of scrub and blackberries to dodge around on the pushbike and at speed it was great fun. Overhead he heard an aeroplane and looked up to see a Tiger Moth Biplane flying very low. Norm was so transfixed he and his bike crashed into a thicket of blackberries. It was very painful extricating himself from the blackberry thorns but from that moment Norm knew what he wanted to do. He wanted to be in that aeroplane. He wanted to fly!

Norm was the youngest of four children in a strongly Protestant family. He had a stocky build with red, curly hair and clear blue eyes. His eyesight was exceptional which would prove an asset flying the dangerous skies over Europe in the 1940's. His father Lindsay Thomas Crouch was a solicitor and partner at the Sydney law firm, J. Stuart Thom & Co. of 45 Market Street, Sydney.

Lindsay Thomas Crouch

Norm's oldest brother John and sister Molly were involved in the Church and his other brother Stuart was to join the family law firm. With responsibilities to family and the Church taken care of and because he was the youngest, Norm was free to do what he wanted. He was always lucky and grew up exploring the vices and virtues of gambling, drinking, mateship and flying.

Norm rushed home, excited to tell his mother about the aeroplane he had seen and to have his scratches tended to. His mother, Mabel Crouch was a quiet, very conservative lady from Dunedin, New Zealand. She had moved to Sydney in

2

1907, at the age of 26 and found work as a secretary at Lindsay's law firm. She and Lindsay fell in love and were married in 1910.

Norm could not contain his excitement about the Tiger Moth. 'Mother I want to fly, that's what I want to do, can you just imagine what it would be like? The freedom, like a bird, to fly.'

Mabel was amused at Norm's excitement but was not going to encourage him. 'Norm, if God had wanted man to fly he would have given him wings. Your father will be home from the office soon. You can talk to him about it at the dinner table.'

Lindsay Thomas Crouch was the head of the family and known to them as 'Papee'. He was strict but also a very kind and generous man. Well regarded as a lawyer he was on the board of a few companies including Coca Cola and there was always a crate of Coke in the garage for the children and grandchildren. If any of his clients were in financial trouble he would let them pay for his services in kind with the result that his house was adorned with many artworks, stuffed animals and Norm's favourite, a genuine black panther rug.

Norm aged 2 and the black panther rug

At the dinner table Papee told Norm he would not encourage or discourage his wanting to fly. He felt at this early stage aviation was a dangerous past time and if he wanted to pursue flying as a career he would have to prove it by paying for lessons and everything himself. Being the youngest child, Norm was a little more spoilt than the other children. Papee had named him after a cousin, Francis Crouch who was killed in the Great War and in memory of Norman Dreyer, a partner in J. Stuart Thom & Co., who also gave his life in the Great War. To Papee, his youngest son's name, Francis Norman, represented sacrifice in war.

Norm's red hair came from his father. Lindsay was born in Bathurst but spent most of his youth in Orange in country New South Wales. He spent several years in the Lands Department in Orange before moving to Sydney to study Law. He was articled to J Stuart Thom & Co. and lived with his uncle, aunt and cousins at The Laythes, Randwick, often running to the city to work. As he could keep pace with the trams, he became known to the regular commuters who called him the 'red runner' because of his crop of red hair. Lindsay joined the firm in 1904 and served as a junior and later, senior partner for 54 years.

After leaving school at 17, Norm was apprenticed as a fitter and turner to Gilbert & Barker who made petrol pumps. He had little interest in the job as all he wanted to do was fly but it did provide him with an income of 17 shillings and 6 pence a week. From his wages 5 shillings went to flying lessons, 5 shillings to his mother, 5 shillings went on fares and the remaining 2 shillings and 6 pence he spent on his passion for crystalized hot ginger and the book 'Learning to Fly' by Frank A Swoffer.

LEARNING TO FLY

The money put aside for flying lessons bought him one hour of instruction on Tiger Moths every two months and in 1937 much to his mother's concern he booked flying lessons with Airflight, a small company operating from Mascot Airfield, which in those days was only a grass field. From his home it was a short walk to Pymble Station where he caught the train to Mascot, crossing over Sydney Harbour on the recently opened Sydney Harbour Bridge. Then a walk across the grass at Mascot to the small Airflight building with a single Tiger Moth parked nearby.

Norm who was only 17, introduced himself to his flying instructor who was an enthusiastic young man in his early twenties. After a long pre-flight inspection of the Tiger Moth, Norm was instructed to sit in the front seat and then shown the controls and instruments. He was given a pair of goggles and a flying helmet with a telephone attached so that the instructor in the back seat could be clearly heard by the pupil in the front seat, above the noise of the engine. Norm then got out and was told how to swing the propeller to start the engine. His instructor jumped into the back seat and shouted, 'Contact,' and Norm swung the propeller. On the third swing the engine started. Norm jumped into the front seat, put his helmet and goggles on and they were away. The Tiger Moth had an open cockpit so the instructor would lean forward and yell his instructions through the helmet telephone to his pupil in front, which on Norm's first flight were to observe the movements of his duplicate controls and not to touch them until told to do so. Norm gave him the 'thumbs up' that he could hear the instructions and understood.

Taxiing to the end of the grass field the instructor turned the aircraft into the wind, gave it full throttle and they were airborne very quickly, climbing above Botany Bay. Norm had never felt more alive and as the little Tiger Moth levelled out and throttled back, he was allowed to try the controls but shortly after the engine started to misfire. The instructor took over the controls and calmly told Norm, 'don't worry, we won't get back to Mascot but we will make that golf course down there.' They were forced into a successful emergency landing on the nearby Lakes Golf Course. It seemed fitting that Norms first flight would end in a forced landing.

In over four years in Bomber Command both on operations and Operational Training Units (OTU), Norm lost count of the number of crashes and crash landings he suffered. He said, 'it was just normal in those days.'

However, nothing dampened his enthusiasm for flying and eventually after one and a half years he completed the necessary eight hours of dual instruction qualifying to fly solo.

On one of his early solo flights he went up to Pymble and did a mild beat up of the family home from 500 ft, he was reported and suspended. Low flying and beat-ups, unauthorised manoeuvres just to cause a stir, were to become a regular habit for him. He loved flying and managed a few more solo hours before the war started.

THE RAAF

On the formal declaration of war on the 3rd September 1939, Norm applied to join the RAAF and was accepted in July 1940. On the 8th August he joined the No.2 Initial Training School (ITS) course at Bradfield Park in Sydney where he was instructed in the theory of flight and Air Force weaponry.

Shortly after completing the course Norm fell ill with German Measles which delayed his progress to Elementary Flying Training by a month. He recovered in the family home at 40 Hope street, Pymble which had been built in 1920, the year he was born. It was a large two-story house with terraced lawns leading down to a clay tennis court on which Norm had spent much time and had become a good club level player with the Hornsby/Killara Tennis Association.

The Pymble home

The property had over three acres of land and they kept a pair of Jersey cows to provide milk for the family. Norm's chore from childhood was to milk the cows. It was in this comfortable and peaceful place, during his recovery, Norm heard via the radio and newspapers of the disturbing news from the war in Europe that the Germans were deliberately bombing civilians in England.

On the 7th September 1940, the Germans launched a massive bombing raid on London using 350 bombers killing or injuring nearly 2,000 people. This was the first day of what became known as the 'The Blitz' where for every day or night for the next eight months, with the exception of only one day, they launched bombing attacks against London, Swansea, Cardiff, Bristol, Southampton, Plymouth, Birmingham, Coventry and Liverpool in an effort to destroy the spirit of the British people. By the end of the Blitz in May 1941, over 32,000 civilians had been killed and 87,000 seriously injured. Two million houses were destroyed.

On his sick bed, Norm had time to think about what his part was going to be in this vicious war. This war where the term 'Total Warfare' was being used for the first time. The Germans had smashed through Europe and in June 1940 had pushed the British Army into the sea at Dunkirk. Norm wondered; would Britain be able to survive? Let alone take the fight back to the enemy who at that time were all conquering. Would the war be over by the time he got to England? He discussed the war situation with his father and family. Initially they were very reluctant to see him go but the news being received of the Germans deliberately targeting civilians with their bombing horrified them and they changed their minds. This Nazi enemy was evil and had to be destroyed. Francis Norman had to represent the family in this war. Norm's brother Stuart wanted to go too but their father, Papee said, 'No! One son is too much to sacrifice for another European War.'

Having recovered, Norm proceeded to Narromine in country New South Wales on the 18th September and joined the No.5 Elementary Flying Training School (EFTS).

Norm was like a lot of the young men who were enlisting in the RAAF at that time. Mainly sons of wealthy and middleclass families, they saw their chances of adventure and gaining commissions much higher as a pilot in the Air Force. They were all volunteers wanting action, adventure and the challenge of facing the enemy in the sky, be it by fighter or bomber. The war was in Europe and they were badly needed there. Japan was not in the war at that time.

At Narromine, Norm joined 50 other trainee pilots but did not disclose he already knew how to fly. He did not want to be held back in Australia as an instructor. He, of course, found it easy and went solo after four hours instruction on Tiger Moths and had fun low flying the country roads forcing vehicle drivers to duck their heads. He would give a friendly wave and a laugh when they jumped from their vehicles and shook their fists at him.

Group photo – EFTS Narromine

On one occasion he was reported for low and dangerous flying but the person making the report put down the wrong time and Norm got off on a technicality. He had been lucky again because he could have been slung out of the Air Force for disobeying orders.

Coventried

'Operation Moonlight Sonata'

Meanwhile, in Europe the war was getting ever more vicious. On the 14th November 1940, which was a beautiful moonlit night in England, the Germans launched 'Operation Moonlight Sonata', a bombing attack on the city of Coventry in the English Midlands with the deliberate intent to destroy the whole city. At 1920 hours, an initial wave of specially modified Heinkel Bombers with the latest navigational aids dropped parachute flares over Coventry acting as pathfinders for the main group of 515 bombers. They bombed all night returning to their base in France to reload, return and bomb again. Coventry was carpet bombed with 30,000 incendiaries and 500 tons of high explosive. They first bombed from the east, then from the west and after 11 hours of sustained bombing much of the city of Coventry was destroyed. The final all clear sounded at 0615 on the morning of 15th November. More than 4,300 homes in Coventry were destroyed and two-thirds of the city's buildings were damaged. The raid was heavily concentrated on the city centre, most of which was destroyed. An estimated 568 people were killed in the raid with many more injured. Casualties were limited by the fact that a large number of the population trekked out of the city after the initial attack to sleep in nearby towns and villages.

Back at their airfields in France the Luftwaffe crews celebrated their destruction of an English city. The Germans only lost one bomber in the whole attack and for the first time had used pathfinder aircraft to mark the targets and used large 'blockbuster bombs' coupled with thousands of incendiary bombs in order to create a firestorm. They thought the raid such a success they boasted they had 'Coventried' Coventry. They would later use that word to describe the damage done by their Bombers against other targets. The German Propaganda Minister Joseph Goebbels used the word, in German, 'coventriet,' to boast of the Luftwaffe's success in this and future attacks.

He would later come to regret it when their own cities were 'Coventried' by Bomber Command Lancasters using similar bomb load tactics but with far greater capacity and effect.

The 50 young men training with Norm on the training course, hearing of the Coventry disaster, were keener than ever to get on the ship to England. They were badly needed because the mother country was in desperate plight and failing on its own. The Russians were still allied with Germany, Europe had been defeated and the USA was not in the war at that time.

After completing their training at Narromine, 40 out of the 50 qualified as pilots would be sent to Canada to take up advanced flying training. Norm had made a few friends in the group including one man who reckoned he could out drink any man from the course. That boast would prove fatal in four months' time on the other side of the world. After Narromine, there was a short embarkation leave and a final chance to go back home to say goodbye to friends and family, before departing to Canada for more training and then England to join an operational squadron.

THE EMPIRE AIR TRAINING SCHEME

In 1939 at the start of the war in England, the RAF realised with great accuracy that to fight this war against the very powerful German enemy they would need 50,000 airmen annually and would only be able to source about half from the United Kingdom. The rest would have to come from the British Empire. The Empire Air Training Scheme was established in December 1939 to train airmen from all around the Empire. The initial elementary flying training was done in their home countries, from there they would travel to Canada to do their advanced flying training. From Canada, they would finally go to the United Kingdom where they joined an operational squadron for the war in Europe.

Norm was in one of the early groups to leave Australia as part of the Empire Air Training Scheme.

Finally, the waiting was over, and on the 22nd February 1941, it was time to go down to Sydney Harbour and board the TSS Awatea for Canada.

Empire Air Training Scheme Airmen leave by 'Awatea' for Canada
(From the collections of the State Library of NSW)

The 'Awatea' was a beautiful ship. Her lovely Maori name meant 'Eye of the Dawn'. In the 1930's this elegant trans-Tasman liner was the fastest and most luxurious ship in the Southern Hemisphere.

Norm said goodbye to his family and a few friends. His father and two older brothers stood strong, shook his hand and wished him luck but his sister Molly could not hold back the tears as she wished him well. His mother Mabel, from the most Scottish of cities, Dunedin N.Z., with her stiff Presbyterian background kissed her youngest son on the cheek and said she would be praying for him. When Norm boarded the ship and was out of earshot she turned to the family and in a matter of fact voice said to them, 'We will never see him again!'

She could have been right. Of all the airmen who left Australia in 1941 and flew with Bomber Command throughout the war, only 8% survived and returned after the war.

Boarding the Awatea that day was Norm's party of 40 trainee pilots and about twice that number of trainee gunners, wireless operators and navigators. Norm's group were travelling first class as, being pilots, it was expected they would get commissions. They would get special treatment wherever they went. There were other passengers including an English Army Colonel from an Indian Regiment and his wife of Indian extraction, who Norm thought was the most beautiful woman he had ever seen.

They were a wonderful pair and good company in the 24 days spent on board the 'Awatea' on the trip to Vancouver. Poker was popular with the pilots and the other first-class passengers and Norm managed to win a lot of money. He was lucky in gambling too. The trainee pilots heading to war had a wonderful trip. They all got to know each other very well and bonded strongly.

On arrival in Vancouver they had to say goodbye to the Colonel and his beautiful wife. They later learned both had been killed when their ship was torpedoed in the Atlantic. The

'Awatea' was also sunk about a year later when she was bombed and torpedoed while landing troops in North Africa.

FLYING TRAINING IN CANADA AND RUNNING GROG

They landed in Vancouver on the west coast of Canada. Their advanced flying training was to be with the No. 1 Service Flying Training School at Camp Borden 80 miles north of Toronto in Eastern Canada. They were put on a troop train which took five days to cross Canada. When they arrived at Camp Borden the Canadians were not ready for them and gave them special passes to stay in Toronto for four days while they waited for the RCAF to be ready to receive them.

They all went to the Royal York Hotel, billed as the biggest hotel in the British Empire, as they were the first Australians to arrive they were given absolute star treatment. They occupied the entire second floor with two to a room and every fourth bedroom was converted to a lounge for their convenience at a special rate of three dollars per person per day.

③

On arrival we were told that we were two days ahead of schedule, so the forty of us were given special passes to Toronto. We went to the Royal York Hotel billed as the biggest hotel in the British Empire. We were the first Australians to arrive and were given absolute star billing. Two to a room and every fourth bedroom converted to a lounge for our convenience. I had won a reasonable sum of money through gambling on the Aquatena, so went to the Hertz car rental office in Toronto and organised a rental Chevrolet for which (believe it or not) I paid 100 dollars per month a special rate for us "Aussies". During my three months there I used the Chev as a taxi and charged 4 of us $1.00 per trip to Toronto every weekend. There was no flying from weekend Friday night to Monday morning. When I first got my car into the Royal York garage the manager of the Hotel came to my room and gave me 500 dollars (a fortune to me) and told me to call into a huge warehouse 50 miles from Toronto. There they loaded crates of whisky gin & brandy into the car and off we went. I'm glad we had no incidents on the road. Toronto was a dry city and the Tani drivers used to bleed the Hotels dry. The money finished at 2000 dollars and our share was one mixed crate of grog. I also saw a lot of Canada including Niagara Falls. Very spell binding.

We flew Yales to start with. Fixed undercarriage not much power. After that on to Harvards. A very sporty single engined fighter. I loved the aircraft but was not very good at acrobatics. Better at navigation though. After 3 months got my wings and an above average assessment but no commission. Just a Flight Sergeant. From there to Montreal where I saw my first circus a high class brothel. Very odd. Then on to Halifax and eventually on to an armed merchantman and a four

Norm's handwritten notes. Arriving in Ontario

With his winnings from the Awatea, Norm decided to hire a car to use as a taxi for his group while they were in Canada and charge $1 each for a trip between the hotel and the airfield at Camp Borden. He went to Hertz and hired a Chevrolet and again because they were the first Aussies, he was given a special rate of $100 per month.

After Norm parked the car in the Royal York Hotel garage the hotel manager came to his room. The manager had a problem supplying alcohol to his hotel. Toronto was almost a dry city and taxis were bleeding the hotel dry. He gave Norm $500 and directions to a huge warehouse 50 miles from Toronto. There they loaded crates of whisky, gin and brandy.

By the end of their three months advanced flying training at Camp Borden, Norm was the hotel's main grog runner and was running over $2,000 of grog per trip, his share was one mixed case of grog for his party. He was also using the Chev as a taxi and every weekend would charge four of his mates $1 each per trip into Toronto.

Back at Camp Borden they flew Yales to start with, a fixed undercarriage aircraft without much power. After that they moved onto Harvards; a very sporty single engine fighter which Norm loved flying but the aircraft was not very good at aerobatics, however it had much better navigation.

Group photo – Camp Borden

After the three months training, at the end of the course, Norm got his wings and an above average assessment but no commission, just a Sergeant. Of the original party of 40 who had left Sydney there were now 37. Two were killed in flying accidents during training. A third who, on successful completion of their flying course, took advantage of their abundance of booze and decided to celebrate by betting he could drink a full bottle of Scotch in 20 seconds. He died and was given a wonderful funeral by his mates.

They left Toronto and went to Montreal for a few days where they visited a high-class brothel which Norm described as being very odd. It was the first and last time for him.

THE CONVOY

From Montreal they travelled to Halifax, Nova Scotia and on the 19th June 1941 they boarded an armed merchantman for the perilous voyage to Scotland. The HMS Ausonia was a liner built for the Cunard Line in 1922 and promptly requisitioned by the Admiralty at the outbreak of the war. It was converted to an armed merchant cruiser and fitted with 8 six-inch guns. They were part of a 40-ship convoy, Convoy HX134, which was re-routed via Iceland in an effort to avoid U-boats which had attacked the previous convoy. Convoy HX133 had departed Halifax just three days earlier and German U-boats had sunk six of their ships.

The young group of Aussies had been together for over four months, they had been treated like kings and spoilt as heroes heading to war. Three members of their party had been killed; they had not been subject to military discipline but were ready for the fight. They had heard unofficial reports from England of the carnage that was happening in Bomber Command and knew that German U-boats were waiting to attack their convoy. They knew their future chance of survival was poor. God help anyone who tried to impose military discipline on them now.

On board the merchantman they were organised into U-boat watches. They each stood three hours on and six hours off. An officer, not from their group, foolishly tried to enforce military discipline organising them into all sorts of compulsory drills. It doesn't last long.

The first few days the convoy was enveloped in thick fog, progress was slow and the ships could not sight each other. The convoy became scattered but they were safe from U-boats in the fog. After two days the fog cleared, the convoy regrouped and the navy escorts took up position patrolling the seas around the convoy. Because they were in the North Atlantic at very high latitude it was light 24 hours a day in the middle of summer but bitterly cold. The three-hour shifts on deck on U-boat watch were freezing particularly when they encountered many North Atlantic gales on the voyage.

There was no respite from watching out for the constant threat of U-boat attacks and with the convoy travelling in daylight all the way and at only six knots they felt they were sitting ducks. It was a terrifying and uncomfortable voyage in complete contrast to their voyage across the warm waters of the Pacific and luxury of the 'Awatea'. Their convoy was lucky and after two weeks it arrived in Iceland without incident. They stayed one week in Iceland before heading to Scotland. They all thought Iceland was a strange place. The locals hated them and thought of them as invaders. The local girls and young women used to bathe naked in the hot springs but with an increasing audience they protected their modesty and started wearing men's speedos to cover their bottoms only.

Their good fortune continued as they also avoided the U-boats on the voyage from Iceland to Scotland and they were relieved when the HMS Ausonia sailed up the Clyde to dock at the Gourock docks. On the 17th July 1941, they disembarked in Scotland and were organised on to a train to the Australian Reception Depot at Bournemouth in Dorset on the sunny southwest coast of England. It was the middle of summer and the weather and countryside were beautiful.

ENGLAND

The group of young Australian pilots had a final two weeks together in beautiful Bournemouth before being dispersed to various units throughout England. They were determined to make the most of this time before being transferred to Operational Training Units. From there they would go to active squadrons where finally their time would come to face the enemy. They had now been together for over five months, had little respect for military discipline and worked as a team to make life hard for the Military Police. Their technique was to befriend the MP's who were trying to move them on from the pubs and entice them to have a friendly beer in sympathy with these Aussies far from home. These Aussies were full of fun but hardened and eventually would get the upper hand by getting the MP's drunk and putting them out onto the street without their clothes. With their three months 'training' in Toronto and access to plentiful alcohol they really knew how to hold their alcohol and the English MP's were no match for them. After this happened twice the group were left alone. Norm, recognisable with his red hair and clear blue eyes was one of the leaders of this gambit. He assumed later that maybe he had got the blame and had a note put on his file– 'troublemaker, never to receive a commission.'

Then the 37 of us (two were killed flying and one dead drank a bottle of Scotch in 20 seconds) went by train to Bournemouth. This was in June 1940 and Bournemouth was beautiful. We had some trouble with the English M.P's but were well organised and they eventually left us alone.

My genuine career started at Stratford on Avon where 12 of us started on Wellington 1A's. Flying was easy but banging was tricky. I can't remember how many hours I logged there because my log books were burnt in a house fire at Eltham after the war, but it wasn't much. From there we were split up and I went to 97 Squadron at Coningsby and its settlest satellite Woodhall Spa. Serving my fourteenth month stay at Woodhall Spa I finished my first and only tour of 200 hours and 36 trips. I started as 2nd pilot to a wonderful bloke called F/Lt Stan Harrison who was half way through his second tour. I flew with Stan for nine trips, the first few being on Manchesters, an aircraft which flew like a dream but its Vulture engines were most unreliable. 44 Squadron and ourselves were the first to be equipped with the Lancaster ① This aircraft was basically a Manchester with 4 Merlin engines and rod controls which made it heavier to fly and was, without doubt, the number one bomber of the whole war. The first Lancaster operation proved to be an absolute fiasco. Just a quiet little gardening job with no opposition but the weather turned bad on the way back. One of the eight Lancs got too close to the Boston cathedral and after a violent steep turn both wing tips fell off and he finished in the WASH with no loss of life. Three two others tried to land back at base (a big party was scheduled) and both crashed, Stan was diverted and landed at Abingdon. The grass was very slippery and we had to fill up the undercarriage. Butch Harris was not amused at a 50% loss. We were off to Augsburg some months later but our aircraft

Norm's handwritten notes. Arrival in England

The end of July saw their group finally split up. The overwhelming majority would be sent to Bomber Command because that's where the need was greatest. Norm with eleven of his mates was assigned to No.22 Operational Training Unit at Wellesbourne Mountford, for training on the Vickers Wellington 1A and 1C medium bombers. Norm was to join Bomber Command.

On the way, on the 1st August at Stratford on Avon, Norm celebrated his 21st birthday and had a lousy birthday alone and far from family.

The Wellington was Norm's first twin engine aircraft and he had a little trouble with taxiing at first but not with flying and passed all courses with above average ratings.

His rank remained as Sergeant.

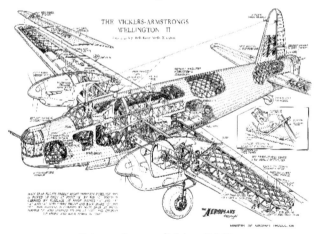

Cutaway image of Vickers Wellington

On the 2nd October 1941, having completed their operational training it was farewell to Norm's final eleven Aussie mates from the Awatea. They were dispersed to operational squadrons throughout Bomber Command. Only 8% would survive the war.

RAF Bomber Command controlled the RAF's bomber forces and at the start of the war was divided into 5 Groups. Numbers 1,2,3,4 and 5. In 1941, each Group comprised between 14 and 21 squadrons with about 12 aircraft per squadron. As the war progressed more groups were added, such as 6 Group which was an all Canadian Group and 8 Group which was a Pathfinder Group. 92 Group was the Operational Training Group.

Norm was posted to 97 Squadron located at Coningsby in Lincolnshire. This was an RAF heavy bomber squadron in 5 Group reformed thanks to a donation from the Government of Malaya. Norm was the first Australian pilot in the squadron, he was noticeable as his blue RAAF uniform contrasted with the blue/grey uniform of the RAF.

Norm, in his RAAF uniform

The time had come to face the enemy.

NORM – BOMBER COMMAND

OPERATIONS AGAINST THE ENEMY

97 Squadron

Norm arrived at Coningsby on the 2nd October 1941. He was made a member of No. 10 crew and was the 2nd Pilot/Flight Engineer to Flight Sergeant Stanley Harrison. Stan was very experienced having just completed his first tour of 30 missions and was dismayed to find his new crew had no operational experience at all. They were a varied lot:

Stan Harrison   Skipper and first pilot from Oxford.

Norm Crouch   2nd. Pilot/Flight Engineer from Sydney.

Dennis Platten   Navigator from Somerset.

George Preston Radio operator from Yorkshire.

George Farara   Bomb aimer/front gunner from Bermuda

Bill Townley   Mid-upper gunner from Toronto, Canada.

Jack Oates   Rear gunner from British Columbia, Canada

Jack Oates, at 30 years of age was the crew's senior citizen and all the others were in their early twenties.

Norm and the new crew introduced themselves and saw their new Bomber for the first time. It was the new and very impressive looking Avro 679 Manchester twin engine heavy bomber capable of carrying a big bomb load all the way to Germany and well defended with three machine gun turrets. Norm was excited, he had arrived at the front line of the war on Germany. Only Bomber Command were able to strike

32

against the Germans who had prevailed everywhere in Europe and were advancing rapidly against Russia, since the surprise attack of Operation Barbarossa in June 1941.

The new crew had four weeks to adapt to their new bomber–the Manchester; with its fuel and hydraulic systems, flying and engine controls, new automatic bombsight, three Frazer Nash hydraulic gun turrets and their multiple machine guns, the enormous bomb bay with its rows of bomb racks and intricate fusing and release mechanisms. Also, the greatly improved radio and intercom systems and the rest bed and chemical toilet within the wide fuselage. This was a far bigger and more complex aircraft than the Wellington.

The Manchester was powered by two Rolls Royce Vulture engines which unfortunately proved to be unreliable.

Training for the crew included cross country flights by day and night, high level bombing, air firing and practicing emergency procedures, particularly engine failure. It didn't take long before they had their first emergency.

With a cloud base of just 1,200 ft they feathered an engine at 1,100 ft. The emergency procedure is needed if an engine fails and requires the three-bladed propeller being rotated to fully coarse pitch or feathered position. The engine should stop with the blade in line with the airstream offering minimum resistance. However, the engine continued to rotate the propeller until it reached fully fine pitch, offering maximum resistance to the airflow and acting as an air brake.

Without enough height to recover they fell to the, fortunately, flat Lincolnshire countryside and crash landed with a resounding, ear piercing sliding crunch as the nose bay, bomb bay and lower fuselage crumpled. They came quickly to a halt in a massive shower of earth, stones and general debris which erupted through the shattered nose. They were all shocked but unhurt and had a fortunate escape. Such accidents were the 'norm' for Bomber Command in those years.

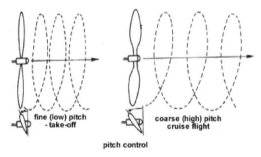

Feathering the Engine - Pitch Control Diagram
(from Pilot Friend)

Finally, with their Manchester training and initiation completed, on the 7th November 1941 No. 10 crew appeared on the 'Operations Tonight' board for the first time. Six and a half months after leaving Australia Norm was to fly his first mission against the enemy.

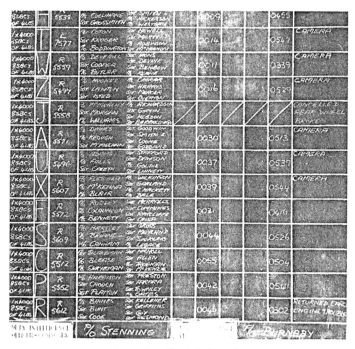

Operations Tonight Board

Their target was German naval vessels in Boulogne Harbour in Northern France and take off time was scheduled for 1740 hours. The totally inexperienced crew were edgy and excited at the prospect of their first mission. Stan, with 30 missions behind him was a calming presence and decided to put his crew's nervous energy to use by boarding their Manchester early at 1600 and keep them busy with comprehensive pre-flight checks. They took off on time. As they approached the French coast and their target, the inexperienced and apprehensive crew were excitedly twittering over the intercom about what they thought they saw in front of them until Stan pointed out the difference between heavy flak bursts and night fighters and/or balloons. They released their ten 500 lb general purpose bombs onto wharves and barges in Boulogne Harbour. A steep turn to starboard took them safely out to mid-channel and they arrived back at Coningsby less than four hours after take-off. A very relieved and jubilant crew were happy with a successful mission to start their tour of duty.

After their first mission, they had a three-week break but were instructed to help prepare for a visit the next week by the King who was coming to inspect the station and the squadron. On the afternoon of the 13th November, King George VI made his inspection and noticing Norm in his blue RAAF uniform said to him, 'You are a long way from home, are you lonely here?'

To which Norm replied, 'No Sir, I like this squadron and they don't mind my sometimes, bad language.' The King laughed and moved on.

They later learned that a week before, on the day of their first operational mission that Bomber Command had despatched 390 heavy bombers, about half to Berlin and others to Cologne, Mannheim, the Ruhr and Channel Ports. Of the 390, no less than 37 had been lost. It meant that 259 Airmen were killed that night.

Indeed, later statistics revealed in the four months from 8 July to 10 November 1941, 414 heavy bombers and 112 light bombers, mainly Blenheims, had been lost, the equivalent of Bomber Command's entire frontline strength in aircraft and crews.

On the 30th November, their second mission was the shipyards at Hamburg. After taking off from Coningsby at 1651 hours, they approached Denmark in very bad weather where they encountered severe icing and were forced to descend to 6,000 ft to avoid it. At that altitude they were met with heavy flak as they crossed from Denmark to the Elbe estuary; to have continued to Hamburg would have been suicidal, so they jettisoned their bombload over the Danish coast and turned for home. However, for the first time they were carrying a vertical camera which was fitted to all heavy bombers to measure the accuracy of their bombing. They were warned at briefings that photo flashes had been known to jam in the flare shute. The flashes were fused to operate just after the bombs hit the ground and contained about 10 lb of very explosive material, enough to blow a large hole in the aircraft. George Farara, the bomb aimer, shouted a warning that the flash was stuck. Norm swore and grabbed a kitchen broom that was nearby and passed it to George and Bill Townley, who had got himself down from the mid-upper gunner's position in record time, and yelled, 'Poke the bloody thing out for Christs sake!'

Meanwhile Stan had put the aircraft in a steep dive then abruptly into a steep climb in a panic-stricken effort to dislodge the flash. After the second dive and climb and with the help of the broom handle George yelled, 'It's gone'. The crew picked themselves up from the floor or ceiling, wherever they had been hurled to and resumed the flight home. This nightmare of a mission wasn't finished. A British ship fired on them as they were heading home. It was a bad mission and they were relieved to get home safely. Norm, already known for his typical Australian bad language exclaimed, 'Our own bloody side is trying to kill us too, what the bloody hell!!'

On 6th December, Norm was promoted to Flight Sergeant, a senior non-commissioned rank in the RAF. Still no commission.

On the 7th December 1941, a major event took place which would alter the course of the war. In the Pacific, the Japanese empire attacked the United States Naval Base at Pearl Harbour bringing America into the war.

The bad weather continued throughout December but despite this they were given a mission on the 7th December to attack the Nazi headquarters in the centre of the town of Aachen. They took off at 0332 and again the weather over north west Europe was atrocious, again they had to retreat with heavy icing as they approached the target. However, they found their secondary target at Calais was clear, so they dropped their bombs on the docks at Calais harbour. Their 4,000 lb bomb was observed to explode on the beach.

The inaccuracy of the night-time bombing caused a change in tactics and after this mission they became aware that Bomber Command had abandoned the pretence of bombing with pinpoint accuracy. From then, carpet bombing or 'area bombing' would be the norm.

For the first time their bomb load included a 4,000-pounder known as a 'cookie'. This was a cylindrical, lightly constructed steel shell packed with RDX high explosive. The 'cookie' was designed to open up factories and buildings and was always accompanied by incendiaries intending to set fire to the wreckage. The usual load was six 500 lb 'cans' of 4 lb incendiaries. This was now the standard bomb load for the heavy bombers of Bomber Command in the offensive against Germany from the end of 1941 to May 1945. The 'area bombing' also meant the Germans at last would get a taste of their own medicine. They had ruthlessly carried out the destruction of British cities during the 'Blitz' and the destruction of European cities like Warsaw and Rotterdam earlier. This way of conducting war, this monstrous battle known as 'Total Warfare' had been joined.

Quoting from Air Marshall Sir Arthur Harris head of Bomber Command:

'The Nazis entered this war under the rather childish delusion that they were going to bomb everyone else, and nobody was going to bomb them. At Rotterdam, London, Warsaw, and half a hundred other places, they put their rather naive theory

into operation. They sowed the wind, and now they are going to reap the whirlwind.'

On December 18th, 97 Squadron provided six Manchesters for a daylight operation on Brest Harbour. No.10 crew were not used. Two very powerful German warships, the battle cruiser Scharnhorst and the heavy cruiser Gneisenau had taken refuge in Brest. For several weeks Bomber Command had tried unsuccessfully to sink the ships to prevent them from raiding the Atlantic convoys. During this attack by 97 Squadron, one of the six Manchesters lost an engine to flak over Brest harbour and as the formation headed out to sea, the stricken aircraft fell behind and was shot down by a Messerschmitt Bf 109. The Manchester was flown by Pilot Officer Stokes, an Australian like Norm serving in the RAF. He was on his first mission and was Norm's first friend to fall in action. The 97 Squadron commander, Wing Commander Balsdon had taken part in this mission, his aircraft had received flak damage over the target and the tail gunner had been shot up. Balsdon had called ahead to have an ambulance waiting and as a result the whole squadron and the Wing Commander's wife waited at Coningsby for the five remaining aircraft to return.

Four eventually returned and landed safely and finally the squadron commander's aircraft was seen on approach. At 100 ft he applied full engine power, presumably having decided to overshoot and try again. But the pilot was not able to regain control and the aircraft went into a steep climb, stalled, plunged into the ground and caught fire. There were no survivors. All this happened in front of the appalled onlookers. It was a terrible blow to the squadron's morale.

Two days later, on the 20th December, a new squadron commander arrived. Wing Commander 'Jack' Kynoch, observing the low morale, decided they all needed firmer discipline and more flying. On Christmas Day when no operations were scheduled they were despatched on a two-and-a-half-hour cross country and bombing exercise before finally being allowed to sit down and enjoy a traditional Christmas dinner. Norm's lack of respect for some military discipline had received more validation and some course language from the remaining Australian pilot in the squadron was heard on that Christmas day.

On the 15th January 1942, their next mission was back to Hamburg. They successfully dropped their bombs on the north-west of town and reported sporadic and inaccurate flak and searchlights. Their homeward route took them north-west and the long sea crossing back to Skegness in Lincolnshire. They had not progressed very far when George Farara, the bomb aimer, pointed out the starboard engine exhausts seemed to be glowing more fiercely than usual and Jack Oates, from the rear turret, reported incandescent sparks were trailing behind the aircraft. The engine was not obviously on fire and in view of the Manchester's poor engine performance and the long way home over water they crossed their fingers and left the bad engine running.

After a seemingly interminable sea crossing, they crossed the coast just south of Skegness and obtained permission from Coningsby Flight Control for an immediate landing. As their wheels touched the ground a brisk fire broke out in the starboard engine. With the main fuel supply turned off they taxied at speed towards the crash fire tender, which doused the engine in foam. The ground crew arrived at the run. With the fire out, the flight sergeant opened the engine cowling and examined the engine; he extended his asbestos gloved hand and the main fuel line disintegrated at his touch.

In the end there was only minutes in it. If the fuel line had fractured while they were in the air the engine would have disappeared in a ball of fire. They were very lucky. After debriefing, Stan said to his crew, 'Norm I've heard you are lucky at cards, maybe you are bringing that luck to my crew. Tomorrow we are off duty and will go to the Blue Bell to celebrate our good luck and survival.'

Next day, in good spirits, they made their way to The Blue Bell Inn on Thorpe Road midway between Coningsby and Woodhall Spa. Built in 1257 in the time of Robin Hood, this old Inn had been the favourite haunt of poachers and hunters and now for the duration of the war was to become a favourite haunt of Bomber Command Aircrews, particularly those from 97 Squadron and 617 and 619 Squadrons. All were based at nearby Woodhall Spa where they were just completing works on building a new airfield with concrete runways, hangars and temporary accommodation for 1,000 men. Woodhall Spa would become a new heavy bomber base and soon home to 97 Squadron.

On the very next day they had some great news. Their first AVRO Lancaster had arrived. For several weeks there had been rumours they were to be re-armed and despite some sightings of a four-engine bomber test flying in the area, it sounded too good to be true. Now with the second prototype Lancaster standing in front of them they learned that 97 Squadron and the African 44 Squadron were the first two Lancaster squadrons and the whole of 5 Group would be so armed in a matter of months.

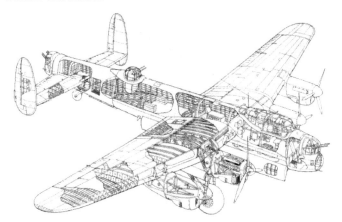

Cross section of the AVRO Lancaster

Lancaster Specifications

Engine:	4 Rolls Royce Packard Merlin 224 V-12's
Wingspan:	102ft
Length:	69ft 6ins
Height:	20ft 4ins
Wing Area:	1300sqft
Maximum Speed:	275 mph
Cruising Speed:	185 to 225 mph
Service Ceiling:	20,000ft (maximum weight)
Maximum Weight:	61,500lbs
Empty Weight:	36,500lbs
Fuel Capacity:	2154 Imperial gallons
Range:	2530 miles with 7,000lb bomb load
	1730 miles with 12,000lb bomb load
	1550 miles with 22,000lb bomb load
Armament:	nose turret - two .303 cal.
	mid-upper turret - two. 303 cal.
	tail turret - four .303 cal.

The Lancaster

The essential difference between the Manchester and the Lancaster was the Manchester had two thoroughly discredited and underpowered Rolls Royce Vulture engines. The Lancaster had four proven, reliable Rolls Royce Merlin engines which were capable of substantial development leading to increased power. To the crews, it was the difference between life and death and their morale rose accordingly!

Norm became the first Australian to pilot the Lancaster. Something he was very proud of, he described it as a 'wonderful' aeroplane. It was a beautiful aircraft to fly, able to be thrown into violent evasive manoeuvres even with a full load. The Lancaster was built to deliver destruction and comfort for the crew played little part in the design. It was so tightly packed with radio and electronic equipment, ammunition for the guns and an enormous bomb load that there was little room for movement and very hard for crew to escape from a stricken aircraft.

The 'compartments' of the wireless operator and the navigator were about two ft square and the noise from the four Merlin engines was overpowering making communication almost impossible without the intercom. The whole aircraft vibrated constantly, at low altitudes it could be stiflingly warm and at the normal operational altitude of 20,000 ft, bitterly cold. Added to this there was the smell of hot oil from which some men became ill aided by the frequent sudden changes in height and direction that most pilots did to evade detection. All this was quite apart from the constant tension and fear from attack and sudden death.

They had one last mission to do in the Manchester. On the 17th January 1942 they took off to attack Bremen, another Naval preserve located on the River Weser, 60 miles west of Hamburg. It was defended by well trained and skilful Naval personnel manning the flak and searchlight batteries. On the way the hydraulic pipe to the rear turret burst so the rear gunner was out of action. Jack Oates called out, 'I cannot protect you from the rear, I'm buggered back here. Are we going on?'

Stan replied, 'Yes we are going on to target. Bill, can you cover Jack's rear position from your mid-upper?'

'Yes skipper, do my best,' Bill Townley called out in his Canadian accent. Good fortune stayed with them and that evening the weather was on their side with broken cloud that discouraged the searchlights and they were able to complete their last Manchester mission without incident.

There was a two-month interlude when their Manchesters were offloaded onto Hampden squadrons who, while happy to dispose of their ancient Hampdens, didn't really want the Manchesters. They were forced to operate them till they too were re-armed with Lancasters. Meanwhile, the crews at 97 Squadron happily collected their new Lancasters from the

AVRO factory at Woodford near the city of Manchester. Their familiarisation with the Lancaster included navigation, bombing and air firing exercises and importantly, low flying exercises.

On the 1st March 1942, 97 Squadron started its move to Woodhall Spa. The ground personnel along with all NCO's and aircrew moved to their new quarters at nearby Tattershall Thorpe, while the officers moved their quarters to the requisitioned officers' mess at the Petwood Hotel, Woodhall Spa.

On the 20th March they were ready for their first Lancaster operation. It was to be a 'gardening' or mine laying operation to lay six sea mines in the sea lanes near Terschelling off the German-Dutch border. It was a daylight operation but the weather was terrible with a cloud base of only 200-300 ft. The whole four-hour journey there and back was flown just above the wave tops.

The mines were successfully laid and after crossing the coast south of Skegness with the cloud base now down to 200 ft and a strong north-easterly gale blowing they made two unsuccessful attempts to land at Coningsby. Flying Control advised them to try for an alternate airfield south-west where the weather was a little clearer. After flying for 30 minutes in that direction, the clouds started to break up and they saw Abingdon airfield which at that time was a small grass airfield.

Desperate to get down because of the weather closing in and because they were exhausted from flying for over four hours at zero altitude in bad weather they landed. But they overshot and applied full brakes but on the saturated grass the brakes had no effect and they were hurtling towards the end of a runway which ended in an open cut quarry. To avert a complete disaster they raised the undercarriage and the aircraft skidded to halt on its belly just short of the quarry. The rear gunner, Jack Oates, was trapped in his turret but his crew mates got him out swiftly and fortunately the aircraft did not catch fire. Crew No.10's first Lancaster sortie in their wonderful new aeroplane did not finish well.

But they did survive, again!

LOW FLYING AND THE AUGSBERG RAID

After a dressing down from Wing Commander Kynoch for poor airmanship in badly damaging a new squadron Lancaster, they were given new instructions to practice low flying at all times. Norm was delighted, he loved low flying and was very skilful as Stan quickly appreciated. Norm could fly his Lancaster below 100 ft, even under power lines. On one occasion a policeman reported him for flying so low that the wingtip of his Lancaster was scraping the ground while banking on the main road into Lincoln. The police were told by the RAF that pilots were following operational orders. On the seventh day of their exercises, low flying in a formation, they completed a six-and-a-half-hour flight which ranged from Selsey Bill on the South Coast to Inverness in Northern Scotland, finishing with a practice bombing attack on the bombing range in The Wash back in Lincolnshire. They correctly surmised that their next mission would take them deep inside Germany.

Bomber Command at this time had a new chief; Bert (Butch) Harris.

The previous month had been very bad news for the Allies. Rommel had recaptured Benghazi; the Japanese, now in the war, had taken Rangoon, had landed in New Guinea and bombed Australia. In the Atlantic, U-boats had sunk nearly half a million tons of

allied shipping. A few more months like that and Britain would be starving. U-boat diesel engines were made at the Maschinenfabrik Augsburg-Nürnberg AG (MAN) diesel factories in Augsburg, situated in Bavaria well inside Germany.

The situation was desperate and Butch Harris formulated a plan to use 12 of the new Lancasters, six each from 44 and 97 Squadrons, on a daring low-level daylight attack on the MAN factories. The sheer audacity of this attack into the German heartland was breathtaking. They would be traversing France and southern Germany for six hours before night fell and very unlikely to avoid the German fighters for that period of time. The crews, on learning the details of the mission, thought it suicidal.

Number 10 crew were assigned to this mission and at 1430 on the 17th April went to their aircraft and started their engines ready for take-off. However, the starboard inner engine was causing problems with a faulty regulating device known as a 'boost capsule' which meant the aircraft would not be able to keep formation. Then George Preston, the wireless operator, found the electric generator to be unserviceable, so they had no choice but to shut the aircraft down. They then watched as the replacement aircraft taxied past and could see its crew looking at them with very glum faces. Number 10 crew had missed a very dodgy operation through providence and or luck.

The next morning they heard the full story of the 'Augsburg Raid'. The 97 and 44 squadrons had operated independently; 44 Squadron had run into the expected swarm of German fighters and four of their six aircraft had been shot down en-route to the target, one more had been lost over the target itself and the only remainder, the formation leader, piloted by Squadron Leader Nettleton, had been badly damaged but managed to get back home. Squadron Leader Nettleton was awarded the Victoria Cross for this operation.

The 97 Squadron had managed to evade the enemy fighters but had lost two aircraft over the target. Of the four 97 Squadron aircraft which survived, one had been badly shot up and lost an engine but to the relief of No. 10 crew, Flying Officer Rodley and his crew, in their replacement aircraft on the raid survived undamaged.

The raid was a success with accurate bombing of the target by those Lancasters that had got through and production of diesel engines for the U-boats halted. The next day the press were lavish in their praise of this daring daylight raid and its success. The surviving crews however were thinking of the seven aircraft and 49 men who did not return. Their teammates and friends violently killed. This was war but to them the price was too high.

By coincidence, on the same day as the daring Augsburg raid, on the other side of the world in the Pacific, another daring and desperate raid was happening. Taking off from aircraft carriers, a force of

USAF B25s led by Colonel Jimmy Doolittle was bombing Tokyo.

The Sunday Pictorial proclaimed the 'Greatest week of bombing in the history of war!' The psychological effect on both Germany and Japan who were at the peak of their powers could not be underestimated.

THE TIRPITZ

After the Augsburg raid, 97 Squadron was stood down for six days. They also had a new Commanding Officer, Wing Commander John Collier DFC (Distinguished Flying Cross). Affectionately known to his fellow officers as 'boy', he set about consolidating the progress made by Wing Commander Kynroch. The 97 Squadron was now rated the no.1 squadron in 5 Group.

On the 23ʳᵈ April, six Lancasters from the squadron, including crew No.10 flew to Lossiemouth in Scotland to join a strike force formed to attack the mighty German battleship 'Tirpitz' hiding in the Trondheim Fjord in Norway. The plan of attack was for Halifaxes to enter the fjord from the North Sea at low level, launching large mines intended to strike the Tirpitz under water and either sink or cripple her. The Lancasters would carry conventional 4,000 lb and 500 lb bombs and drop them from about 8000 ft. drawing fire from the Tirpitz's guns allowing the Halifaxes to come in low with their mines. The attack was scheduled for 24ᵗʰ April but on that night and the following two nights, the weather was bad and the mission was postponed.

The crews decided to let their hair down and on each of the free evenings they 'invaded' the small market town of Elgin. They transformed this normally very quiet Scottish town into a rowdy, drunken festival. They bellowed their squadron songs, loudly trying to outdo each other, plastering their squadron logos over the walls and ceilings of the towns hotels and pubs and generally taking over the place. However, it was all good-humoured fun; there were no fights, no damage. Just young men having a good time because they knew that many of them would not survive long in this deadly air war.

On the 27th April the weather improved and the first attack was launched. Crew No. 10's Lancaster was in the force being held back to attack next day if the first attack was unsuccessful, which it was. Not a single bomb had hit the Tirpitz. Next day, the 28th April, they took off at 2100. Their force consisted of 11 Lancasters followed by 23 Halifaxes. Norm's Lancaster found the night clear over the target except for haze from a smoke screen. They dropped their bombs from 8,000 ft and straddled the ship but did not get a direct hit. The searchlights were active and they were held in their beam for several minutes but luckily avoided the flak that was both heavy and accurate.

They decided to loiter at about 5,000 ft out of harm's way and watch the Halifaxes press home their attack. Because of the now very effective smoke screen which was hiding the target, they changed tactics and instead of trying to directly attack the ship with their mines, the Halifaxes dropped their mines on the steep hillside above the Tirpitz hoping they would roll down the hill and strike the ship. But what happened was the mines got caught up on trees and rocks and exploded harmlessly on the side of the mountain. The Tirpitz remained undamaged but never escaped from the fjord and was destroyed by bombing two years later. Four Halifaxes and one Lancaster were lost in this operation. Another 35 airmen did not survive.

The following day, the crews returned to their home bases and were all given severe reprimands by their CO's for the riotous behaviour in Elgin. But in light of the losses suffered on that occasion and on the Augsburg raid a week earlier, who could fairly point a finger?

The losses kept coming for 97 Squadron. Just three days later, on May 1st, the squadron was practicing formation flying when it came under mock attack from a local Fighter Operational Training Group. This was a normal arrangement between the fighter and bomber groups and it also gave the bombers' gunners useful sighting practice. The mock attacks were usually from astern. On this occasion they were flying as no.2 in the formation and spotted a Spitfire above and in front preparing to make a head on pass. This time the Spitfire did not break off the attack and struck the no.3 Lancaster in the formation head-on, and with its port wing leading edge, sliced off the outer 10 ft of the Lancaster's starboard wing. The Spitfire then cartwheeled to their rear and broke up. The no.3 Lancaster, which was only about 100 ft to their left, slowly rolled over to her right, the nose dropped, and the inverted aircraft dived into the ground a minute or so later and exploded. No reason was ever found to explain this tragic loss of seven of their friends lives and one student Spitfire pilot. The whole squadron felt sickened by the incident.

THE FIRST 1,000 BOMBER RAID – COLOGNE
'COVENTRIED'

Norm was to fly five more missions as no.2 to Stan Harrison who was later transferred to an Operational Training Unit (OTU) to train crews up to Lancaster standard. Norm would take over as skipper of No.10 crew and both Stan and Norm were quite happy at this prospect. One of those five missions was the first 1,000 bomber raid when 1,047 bombers attacked the City of Cologne on 30th and 31st May 1942.

Air Chief Marshall Harris devoted the entire strength of Bomber Command, plus all capable bombers from Training Command and anywhere else that could supply an airworthy bomber, for this one massive raid. All went to plan and as they approached Cologne in the bright moonlight, they could see an unprecedented number of fires which appeared to form into one enormous conflagration, as the city was showered by many thousands of incendiaries interspersed with 'cookies', 500 lb and 1,000 lb bombs. They released their 'cookie' and eight containers of incendiaries on a southern suburb, the target allotted to 5 Group.

They stared fascinated at the sight of a city of one million people being destroyed by fire. The heavy flak from the flak gunners below and the searchlight batteries was inaccurate due to the enormous destruction enveloping them on the ground. As they turned for home they could look back and see the bright red glow in the eastern sky more than 50 miles behind them.

This, for the first time, displayed the enormous destructive power Bomber Command was now capable of. Its effect on the public and the powers that be was equally dramatic. For four years the Germans had bombed their way through the cities of Europe and Great Britain with little retaliation, now at last it seemed like the fightback had started. From that night onwards, the Bomber Command policy of area bombing leading to the destruction of German cities and towns was relentlessly pursued.

When they landed home at Woodhall Spa their sense of euphoria was communicated to the ground crew, to the Operations Room staff and across the whole station. The fact that 41 aircraft had been lost did not detract from the heady feeling of victory. At last there was confidence they could win the war and it would be Bomber Command that would do most to force the Germans to surrender.

TAKING OVER AS SKIPPER

In June, No. 10 crew lost their original navigator, Dennis Platten. He had flown 11 missions with them but was lent to another aircraft for a mission from which it did not return. Dennis was replaced by a navigator, B. Cook and they gained a genuine flight-engineer, Sergeant W. Whittaker, Norm's replacement, when Norm took over as skipper from Stan Harrison.

Shortly after Norm took over the crew, his rear gunner, Jack Oates, frustrated at his gun turret fogging up, got a hacksaw and cut a large hole in the Perspex so he could see better. Norm's Lancaster and crew were then sent to Farnborough to enable the aircraft's designers to evaluate how this affected the aerodynamics of the Lancaster. The trip was supposed to be for one day only, but eventually took a week. They were booked into the Queens Hotel at Aldershot which the military had taken over to accommodate army officers, the lowest rank there was Lieutenant Colonel.

During the next eight or nine months, did some good and some very bad trips. Got holed four or five times. Towards the end was 1st in Bomber Command for 2 months in a row and second the 3rd month. A New Zealander w/o ballinanes was second in the 2 months, and first on the 3rd month. This put 97 Squadron as No 1 Squadron in all of Bomber Command.

My crew were terrific. 3 Canadians, 1 West Indian, 1 English, 1 Australian. All N.C.O's. My rear gunner was Jack Oaks who was 11 years older than the rest of us. Jack got fed up with the rear turret fogging up, so got a hacksaw blade and cut a large hole in the perspex. We went down to Farnborough to get an evaluation on the aerodynamics of the rear turret and stayed a week. We were booked into the Queens Hotel at Aldershot where the lowest rank was a Lt/colonel. During dinner one of the Generals aides (there were 6 generals) asked if we were on operations. On answering yes we spent the rest of the week under their patronage.

When we had only three trips to go, our CO left and we got a new broom who decided to change everything. During the next two months we went from No 1 to No 21 (there were only 21 Squadrons in Five Group). Being the longest living man on the Squadron because during the last few months we had lost the Squadron well over twice, I went to the C.O. and told him that his stupid ideas had completely ruined the Squadron and he should resign. Next morning I was at Brighton in a new Disciplinary course. Lots of Canadians and Australians, very few others. The first few days were hard, up at 6 am lights out 8 pm, P.T. and drilling all day. However, after a few days we found that our corporal Instructor was on our side and the next 10 days were terrific. The exit door opened for 30 seconds after 8 pm and the only door did the same just before 6 am. Back to the Squadron after a brief visit to Australia

Norm's handwritten notes. His crew.

At dinner on the first night, a General's aide asked if they were there on operations. On replying, 'Yes,' they spent the rest of the week under the General's patronage and were spoilt rotten. It was a wonderful break from the horrors of the Ruhr night-time raids against the increasingly capable German defences.

At the conclusion of their week in Farnborough, the Lancaster's designers found no adverse effect was caused to the aircraft's aerodynamics. The only difference being that the rear turret was about two degrees colder but it was thought to be well worth it for the gunner to have a clear line of sight. Many other gunners then did the same, cutting a semi-circular hole in the front of the turret. However shortly after, an official modification came off the assembly line, where the front panel was mounted on side grooves allowing it to be dropped to give a clear view and the problem was solved.

On the 6th June, Norm was promoted to Warrant Officer, still no commission.

Later, he was offered a commission and a promotion to Flight Lieutenant to transfer to 460 squadron, which was an Australian squadron. He refused the promotion and transfer because he loved 97 Squadron and enjoyed the rank of Warrant Officer. Norm had topped Bomber Command for bombing accuracy two months in a row and second in the third month to a New Zealander, W/O Cullinane also of 97 Squadron. Cullinane had also been second to Norm in the two months when Norm had come first. They were judged by the best target aiming point photos. 97 Squadron was ranked no.1 out of the 21 squadrons in 5 Group for most of this time and Norm was proud to serve in the no.1 ranked squadron.

In the next nine months Norm would complete another 25 missions with his crew. They were all NCO's and a great crew. Some missions were routine but most were very bad, being mainly attacks on the heavily defended Ruhr valley, the heart of the German Industrial machine and the most heavily defended target of all. The Ruhr was referred to by aircrew as 'Happy Valley'.

It was during this time that 97 Squadron had another inspection from King George VI. He recognised Norm and said to him, 'Are you still here?'

To which Norm replied, 'Yes Sir, they haven't got me yet.'

NORM – BOMBER COMMAND

GARDENING – MINELAYING

Minelaying by aircraft demands navigation of the highest order because the spots specified by the Admiralty to place the mines must be found in the dark, without the benefit of landmarks. Gardening was the code word for minelaying, a technique with a silent glide approach, almost at wave level, before dropping the huge mines by parachute. Silence was essential because the operation usually meant an excursion into the enemy's heavily defended backyard where land batteries and flak ships were always ready for them.

So far Norm had flown four 'gardening' operations and had successfully laid his mines without incident. However, one of their worst missions to date was to be on the 16th August 1942. They took off from Woodhall Spa at 2155 bound for the Kiel Canal in Denmark on a 'gardening' operation. The conditions were poor with low cloud and poor visibility. The enemy heard them and their Lancaster was caught in searchlights which were then shot out by the tail gunner Flight Sergeant Oates and mid-upper gunner Bill Townley. They were still holed by a couple of exploding canon shells and their port engine was shot out but went on and laid their mines in the correct place. They made it back to base and counted 300 holes, mainly about the roof and mid fuselage, with a large piece of shrapnel missing Bill Townley in the mid-upper gunner's seat by a quarter of an inch. Their aircraft was a mess and once again the crew wondered at their luck in returning uninjured.

KASSEL

Two missions later they had an even more terrifying operation. On the evening of the 27th August, the Operations Tonight board listed Norm's crew and their target was Kassel.

Kassel is a city in Central Germany and was home to the Feiseler Aircraft Plant producing Messerschmitt bf.109 fighter aircraft and Focke Wulf 190 fighters. It was also home to the massive Henschel & Sohns factories producing tiger tanks, engines, vehicles and locomotives. Because of the importance of these factories to the German war effort, Kassel had some of the strongest defences of any German city. At the pre-flight briefing they were told what their target was and were warned the German defences were very strong. That night would be a major effort by Bomber Command using 306 bombers to try and totally destroy this facility. The 97 Squadron would provide six Lancasters.

They took off from Woodhall Spa at 2103 hours and set course for Germany. As they crossed France and were getting closer to Germany they realised it was a beautiful clear night and their apprehension grew. There wouldn't be any cloud to throw off the guns and searchlights or to hide from the night fighters. This trip was going to be bad. They all felt it.

They continued on and were soon into Germany, the target was getting closer. The darkness ahead was lit by many shafts of white light, as searchlights reached up and searched the sky. At their base, flames of red and orange with green and blue edges lit up the darkness as the bombers in front dropped their incendiaries and buildings and vehicles burned. Light flak, coloured red and green and yellow, was reaching up towards them and a searchlight passed over them for a few seconds immersing them in brilliant white light before heavy flak shells burst near them and buffeted their aircraft. The intensity of the flak was incredible.

Brian Cook, the navigator, yelled, 'Three minutes,' and the gunners were yelling, 'Weave, weave for Christ's sake.' They were just as likely to weave into a flak shell and George Ferara, the Bomb-aimer, was now calling to keep straight on as they approached the target. Flak was bursting all around them and they could smell the cordite from the explosions. The aircraft was bucking up and down and Norm was struggling to hold it steady. They were flying into a box barrage, a barrage of anti-aircraft fire intended to block off invaders from a given objective and there was no point of evasion. The sky ahead was lit with white, yellow and red explosions and the sound of metal shrapnel hitting the fuselage was like hail on a tin roof. Norm couldn't see a way through, they were flying through drifting clouds of smoke at 16,000 ft. They were going to need all their luck tonight.

George, the Bomb-aimer, called, 'One minute, right, right, left a little, that's it, steady, steady, steady, bombs gone.' Without the weight of the bombs the aircraft suddenly went up like a lift. Bill Townley, in the middle-upper gunner turret, shouted a warning as the shadow of a night fighter passed behind them. Norm put the Lancaster's nose down into a corkscrew dive to pick up speed and get the hell out of there and shake off any night fighters who may be lining them up. Then a searchlight caught them and held them, then a second and a third and they were coned and blinded in the glare. Norm threw the Lancaster around the sky still gathering speed and diving. They were a lit and an exposed target taking cannon fire and 12 shells passed through the aircraft without exploding.

Their rapid loss of height had tricked the explosive canon shells which were fused to explode at a higher altitude. For what seemed over 10 minutes, they were coned and the Lancaster was now doing 350 mph in a steady dive but unable to escape the enormous and skilful German defences. Norm in desperation yelled to his crew, 'Hold on,' and turned the aircraft on its back into a vertical dive determined to shake off the searchlights even if it meant ripping the wings off. They were going to get blown out of the sky anyway!

The Lancaster was now doing over 400 mph which was well over its limit. Suddenly they had broken through and were in darkness again and Norm was able to recover from the dive at about 3,000 ft and level off. The searchlights and cannons were behind them. They had escaped and were now flying at 300 mph and at about 1,000 ft above the ground, praying the German night fighters hadn't picked them up when they were in the lights. After 15 minutes and with the course set for home, they started to relax. The rest of the journey was uneventful, and they landed back at Woodhall Spa at 0216 in the knowledge they had been very lucky to survive. They went straight to debriefing and then to bed. This time they did not stay to check the holes and damage to their Lancaster. It could wait until morning and the daylight. Being shot up was no longer a novelty to them. The screaming upside-down vertical dive through the blinding light and exploding cannon shells would give Norm nightmares in later years.

On the 10th September, Wing Commander Graham Jones DFC joined 97 Squadron to take over as Commanding Officer from Wing Commander Collier who had succeeded in making 97 Squadron the top-ranking squadron in 5 Group. In recognition of his efforts Wing Commander Collier was awarded the Distinguished Service Order (DSO) and posted to the RAF Staff College at Gerrards Cross. Norm and other senior crews were sad to lose 'boy' Collier who was widely liked and respected.

Wing Commander Jones was different. He was a quiet man with a slow drawl, who only spoke to say something important. He had gained a reputation in 211 Squadron as being a naturally cautious airman, whose chief ambition was to keep his flight intact. He insisted on leading 97 Squadron on a number of very dangerous raids and his personal courage could not be questioned. Norm, however, was concerned that his 'clean broom' approach to the administration of the squadron, including the mixing up of some crews, caused it to fall from its no.1 ranking to no. 21; there were only 21 Squadrons in 5 Group. Norm had been very proud to be flying with 97 Squadron with its no. 1 ranking in 5 Group and was getting angry.

BRIGHTON DISCIPLINARY UNIT

By the middle of October 1942, Norm was the most senior pilot left alive. During the previous 10 months, they had lost the squadron more than twice over. Despite having only one more mission to fly before completing his tour, he felt it was his responsibility to confront the Wing Commander and tell him his stupid ideas had completely destroyed the squadron and he should resign. The Wing Commander was furious that this Australian W.O. in his blue RAAF uniform was giving him a dressing down and in colourful language too. Norm's red hair and blue eyes were accentuated by his temper in their confrontation. The Wing Commander would ensure that at last, this Australian would receive some overdue British Military discipline.

The next morning, at the old Albion Hotel in Brighton which had been converted by the RAF into a secured disciplinary unit, Warrant Officer Norm Crouch arrived; despite his record of 37 completed missions, being the most experienced pilot in 97 Squadron and also a recommendation for the Distinguished Flying Medal (DFM) to start his forced disciplinary course. Most of the others on the disciplinary course were Australians and some Canadians but few other nationalities. The first few days were hard; up at 0600, lights out at 2000, and they were locked in. There was physical training and drilling from dawn to dusk, being yelled at and insulted by a particularly aggressive Sergeant Drill Instructor who seemed to have a hatred of Australians and Canadians.

After a few days they found that a Corporal Instructor was sympathetic to them and on their side and for the next ten days the exit doors opened for 30 seconds after 2000 and the entry door did the same just before 0600. After that they had a great time in Brighton. At the completion of the course Norm, along with other Australians and Canadians made a visit to Australia House (Canada House to the Canadians) in London and claimed victimisation against one Sergeant Instructor from the course who Norm thought was a proper sadist. The result was the drill Sergeant lost his stripes. Norm then returned to 97 Squadron and reported to the Wing Commander. When he was asked if the course had done him any good Norm replied, 'No, but I had a great time.' The Wing Commander in exasperation told Norm, 'Then you can go back and do another two weeks.' Next morning Norm was back at Brighton Disciplinary School and only did two days there before a Humber staff car came and picked him up and returned him to his squadron. The Wing Commander was not there to greet him.

LAST MISSION

By this time, Norm had done 37 missions and had one more to do before completing his tour. The rest of his crew had finished their tour. They were all NCO's and had been a great crew and importantly, a lucky crew together. Despite their aircraft being holed on many occasions and on one occasion losing two engines on the same side at take-off with a full bomb load which was very hairy, by some miracle they had survived without injury.

On the 7th November 1942 at 1738 hours, Norm took off on his final mission with a new crew to bomb the docks in Genoa, Italy. This was to be a 10 hour round trip across Switzerland and over the Alps. About 20 miles from Geneva the outer port engine of their Lancaster caught fire, Norm used the fire extinguisher and shut it down. They were losing height over high ground, so Norm jettisoned their bomb load over open country in Switzerland and turned around and headed back. About one hour from home and still over enemy country they lost a second engine, however their Lancaster, wonderful aircraft that it was, got them home to Woodhall Spa at three minutes after midnight. For the second time, Norm had returned on only two engines. Although his last mission had not been successful Norm was satisfied and relieved his tour was over. He was 'fed up' with being shot up and bid farewell to 97 Squadron, a Squadron he had loved being a part of. It was the last time Norm would fly the Lancaster.

At the end of the war Sir Arthur Harris said, 'As the user of the Lancaster during the last three and a one-half years of bitter, unrelenting warfare, I would say this to those who placed that shining sword in our hands; without your genius and your effort, we would not have prevailed–the Lancaster was the greatest single factor in winning the war.'

92 GROUP – TRAINING COMMAND

Drane Lowe

From Woodhall Spa and 97 Squadron and after a short leave, Norm was posted to 14 Operational Training Unit at Desborough. This was one of many in 92 Group, there he would fly Wellingtons and train new crews to operational standard.

He reported to his new CO, Group Captain Drane Lowe CBE DFC AFC, who was a very dapper man with a moustache and looked like a RAF Group Captain should. Drane had joined the RAF in August 1935 and was posted to 49 Squadron flying Hawker Hinds as a light bomber. At the outbreak of the war he took part in bombing raids over France, flying Hampdens, then Wellingtons on missions over occupied Europe. Fully operational until mid-1941, he was then posted to a commanding rank in 92 Group the Training Command.

He was straightforward and had a twinkle in his eye and Norm liked him immediately. Looking at Norm's file Drane had noted lapses of military discipline and the recent visits to the Brighton Disciplinary School. He also noted the recommendation for the Distinguished Flying Medal (DFM), the 38 missions, many against the heavily defended Ruhr and the fact that despite heavy damage on numerous occasions Norm had always brought his aircraft home with his crew uninjured. Drane wanted this sort of man to teach his student pilots. However, he knew Norm reacted negatively to over-discipline and he did not want to create a rebel under his command. He needed to be firm but fair.

OTU 1943 Norm back left. Group Captain Drane Lowe centre front

Norm became a category 'A2' instructor and was graded 'exceptional'.

Drane was honest and respectful when he told Norm that instructing at an OTU was just as likely to get him killed as flying operational missions. Because of the heavy losses in Bomber Command, the pressure to get new crews trained and operational was high, particularly in winter. OTU's were losing about four crews crashing out of a course of 16.

'These are your new orders and you have no choice in the matter. I need to have an Australian join my team because I do have an additional requirement from you.' Norm raised his eyebrows. Drane explained, 'On Tuesdays, at a Cemetery near

Cambridge, we bury aircrew from 92 Group who have been killed. I would like you to oversee and attend the funerals of any Australians.'

'Yes Sir of course, an honour to do that,' said Norm.

'As a reward you will have a night in London on the return trip,' said Drane.

'Yes Sir.'

From that day, Group Captain Drane Lowe and W/O Norm Crouch became good friends. Norm had also made a good friend in Joe Coombes, another pilot instructor in the Unit. Joe was a very odd person and a complete genius. He had four red endorsements and five green in his logbook. The reds were for crashing when he was drunk and the greens were for rescuing pupils when they were lost above low cloud near the aerodrome. Joe would fly up through the cloud and lead the lost pupil back down through the cloud and appear right above the aerodrome. He had an amazing time clock in his head. Whenever Drane was transferred to take charge of another OTU Norm, Joe Coombes and the station cook would go with him. This team, this partnership, this friendship, continued for two and a half years. The remainder of the war.

On 1st January 1943, Norm was awarded his Distinguished Flying Medal.

The citation read, 'Flight Sergeant Crouch as captain of aircraft has taken part in many operational missions, the majority of which have been against the heavily defended targets in the Ruhr and Western Germany. He has set a fine example to all by his courage and determination.'

The award appeared in the London Gazette on 8th January 1943. The DFM was awarded only to NCO's and was relatively rare being awarded for exceptional valour, courage, or devotion to duty while flying in active operations against the enemy. Norm was very proud of this recognition but he was almost killed before he could be awarded his medal.

On the 23rd January at 0940 hours, Norm took off from Harlaxton Landing Ground with five trainees in his Wellington. They were a mix of pilots, navigators, bomb-aimers and air-gunners. Suddenly, a few minutes after take-off, the starboard engine seized, part of which hit the tailplane, the aircraft went upside down and crashed. Norm, having been a mad surfer on the Northern beaches of Sydney, knew the only way to escape unharmed when a huge dumper got you was to curl up in a ball and relax. He did just that and was slung out of the aircraft, went through the armour plating and finished up past the wing. All he got was a broken nose, a laceration of his knee and massive bruising on his back. The other crew were all injured on impact, the Wellington caught fire and was destroyed. Norm, extremely lucky once again, was in Rauceby Hospital for a month after the crash mainly because of the damage to his back, and because his surgeon, Mr Archibald McIndoe, wanted to reshape his broken nose.

While Norm was in hospital on the 18th February 1943, the German Propaganda Minister Joseph Goebbels made a speech to the German people exhorting 'Total Warfare' and for all civilians to join the war effort. This famous speech was delivered to rapturous applause from his large audience at the Berlin Sportpalast and broadcast by radio to the German population.

The speech was delivered just after the German defeat at Stalingrad when the war was turning against Germany. Norm reflected on the last time he had been on a sick bed, at home in Pymble in 1940 and first heard of the ruthless German military machine employing total warfare and deliberately bombing civilians. He realised now, three years later, the Nazis were still calling for total warfare and only the total destruction of Germany and the Nazi Regime would win the war. There could be no mercy and Bomber Command along with the U.S. 8th. Air Force would have to do most of the destruction. You could not come second in total warfare.

MARGERY

Shortly after recovering, Norm had another crash in a Wellington. On that occasion it was only a mild crash after another engine failure. He had a staff master gunner and eleven trainee gunners on board and finished up crash landing in a field. He got out as quick as he could and found the twelve gunners waiting for him outside. An ambulance came and took the gunners but didn't have room for Norm. Norm said he was okay and could wait. The driver told him he would send another ambulance. Norm sat on the wing of the crashed Wellington bomber and waited.

About an hour later he saw an ambulance approaching through the fields. The driver got out and said, 'I am sorry it took me so long. It was hard to find. Are you alright?' Norm was dumb struck for a few seconds. The ambulance driver was a woman, a very beautiful woman, dressed in her neat WAAF uniform in the rank of Leading Aircraft Woman (LACW). Concerned his silence may mean he was concussed she called again, 'Are you ok? My name is Margery and I have come to take you back to your unit. I am also with 14 OTU and Group Captain Lowe is concerned that you are okay after your bad crash recently. He sent me to bring you back.'

Margery in Uniform

Norm thought, 'Thank you Drane, thank you.' He found his voice and though initially, he was going to make light of his injuries as he did with the first ambulance, he quickly decided he would like some tender care from Margery. 'My back is sore and I may have damaged my knee again, can you help me to the ambulance?' With Norm's arm over her shoulder and Margery's arm around his waist supporting his weight, Norm hobbled to the ambulance. It was an act but Norm wasn't letting on.

Margery Morwood was a farmers' daughter from Kettleby Thorpe Farm three miles from Brigg in Northern Lincolnshire. She had learned to drive the tractor and her father's car while helping around the farm. Every week she would drive her father, James Morwood to Brigg on market day. When she joined the WAAF on 8th December 1941, she went into medical and because she could drive became a nurse and ambulance driver. She was 23 years old, 5 ft 3 inches tall, brunette and the local beauty. Her boyfriend, George Gurnell, a local teacher was anxious to become engaged and boasted Margery had the best legs in Lincolnshire. Norm, who was smitten, ensured he stayed in the sick bay as long as possible and allowed Margery to nurse him. Margery liked him and found him to be fun and very cheeky. She eventually agreed to go out with him to a movie and they saw Ronald Colman and Greer Garson in 'Random Harvest'. Their romance bloomed in the months that followed while they were together in 14 OTU under the kind eye of Group Captain Drane Lowe.

DAM BUSTERS

During the time Norm was recovering from the crash, he had a visit from two friends, Micky Martin from 50 Squadron and Joe McCarthy from his old 97 Squadron. They were a contrasting couple. Flight Lieutenant Micky Martin was from Sydney, like Norm, and was small and dark haired with a large black moustache. Pilot Officer Joe McCarthy was a big blonde, man, an American from Brooklyn who had served as a lifeguard on Coney Island before going to Ottawa and joining the RCAF because he wanted to see some action. Joe had joined 97 Squadron in September and had struck up a friendship with Norm who was then the senior pilot left alive at the squadron. Joe was one of the reasons Norm liked the Americans so much. Micky Martin was recruiting for a new squadron and was looking for pilots skilled at low flying. Micky himself was an advocate for low flying and had found if you flew lower than the other bombers you would avoid the enemy fighters, even lower still the heavy flak would explode above you, and if you flew very low at treetop height you would be gone before the light flak could react. The main danger remaining would be barrage balloons with their steel cables. Micky reasoned there wouldn't be any balloons along main roads or railway lines so he followed those. He and Norm had many conversations about their shared love of low flying. His friends were keen to have Norm join but were unable to give any details about the new squadron, other than it was being led by Wing Commander Guy Gibson and everything was very secret. Norm did not like Guy Gibson though he admired his courage. He was a strict enforcer of military discipline and Norm thought he was a pain in the neck. You could not walk past him without saluting. Norm declined the offer to join what became known as the Dambuster's Squadron. Two months later, on the 17th May came the news 617 Squadron had breached the giant Möhne and Edersee Dams in Germany. It sent over 300 million tons of water crashing into the valleys of the Ruhr causing enormous destruction to Germany's industrial heart. Micky Martin had been successful in helping destroy the Möhne Dam. Joe McCarthy successfully bombed the Sorpe Dam and saw that 50 yards of its crest had crumbled after his attack but unfortunately there were no more aircraft to follow up and though that dam was damaged it was not breached. They both survived the raid and of the 19 Lancaster bombers used for the attack, eight were lost, 53 airmen were killed and three were captured.

STUART CROUCH

In April 1943, Norm's brother Stuart arrived unexpectantly at his OTU. Since Norm had left for the war in February 1941, back in Australia, Stuart had been urging his father to let him go too. Stuart was frustrated at being stuck in Sydney studying for his law degree while his young brother was already in Canada doing his advanced flying training. Despite Stuart having only one more exam to pass his law degree, Papee relented and Stuart joined the RAAF on 31st March 1941. In December 1941, Japan attacked the American fleet in Pearl Harbour and suddenly Australia was put under direct threat from the Japanese. Stuart at that time had just finished his advanced flying training in Canada and was held in Nova Scotia pending a decision from the authorities whether to return his group to Australia to meet the Japanese menace or to send them on to England. The politicians saw Germany as a greater threat than Japan and decided to send the group on to the European war. Meanwhile in Australia, the oldest brother John had an essential wartime job with Union Carbide and could not be released, therefore sparing one of Papee's boys from the war.

Japan was rapidly expanding through Asia and the Pacific. Their submarines had attacked Sydney and Newcastle and Darwin was being bombed and in New Guinea the family had their first loss of the war. In 1942, Molly Crouch married an army officer, Lieutenant Reginald William Hough (Bill), who was in the 58/59th Australia Militia Battalion and was posted to New Guinea.

On the 1st August 1943, in the battle of Salamaua, Lieutenant Bill Hough with his Batman went out to reconnoitre a Japanese machine gun position. Only the Batman returned. Mollie had given birth to a baby boy, Ian, while Bill was training in Australia. She had been diligent in following Bill around the country to be near his training grounds so he would have an opportunity to see his son before being sent to war. She succeeded, and at 3 months of age a sleeping Ian was held by his father. Shortly after, Bill was sent to New Guinea to fight the Japanese. Bill never saw his son again and Ian never knew his father. Lieutenant Reginald William Hough's headstone is in the beautiful tropical grounds of the Lae War Cemetery.

Stuart, like Norm before him left Halifax and avoided the U-boats in the North Atlantic reaching England and by coincidence was sent to Norm's OTU. Stuart got through his operational training with Norm as his instructor. Norm spent many additional hours training Stuart and passed on everything he had learned during his 38 operational missions. He knew experience greatly increased the chances of survival in Bomber Command and taught his brother all the tricks he knew. Stuart's operational tour was then delayed for quite a long while over some incident he himself defended and won. Norm and Margery were courting and over the months ahead,

Stuart accompanied them to many parties and pubs. There was much fun and laughter, young men and women together trying to enjoy life and forget the carnage in Bomber Command that was killing their friends every day. Before leaving Australia, Stuart had married Mary Slater who lived with him for the three months of his initial flying training in Temora NSW.

Now in England, Stuart restricted himself from female company because he was a very responsible man. He became lonely among his aircrew friends enjoying themselves. There were always parties and dances, young men and women enjoying themselves. Every six weeks aircrew were awarded six days leave. To live until their next leave became the greatest hope for each of them and they were determined to enjoy it. One evening they were at the Saracens Head Hotel in Lincoln, a favourite place for Bomber aircrews and known as the 'snake pit'. Margery introduced Stuart to a WAAF friend, Jenny. Stuart was very charming and Jenny fell in love with him. Stuart and Jenny were very happy and spent the rest of the war together.

Norm & Stuart – Kettleby Farm

Stuart knew he had almost no chance of surviving and returning to Australia and like all Bomber Command aircrew lived for the present because they could not count on there being a future. He and Jenny had found comfort and love and were happy for the duration of the war.

Stuart joined 463 Squadron, an Australian squadron operating out of nearby Waddington, and did a full tour on Lancasters. At that time of the war, in Bomber Command, the 'chop rate' was 92% for those who went through OTU and did a full tour. It must have been rare for two brothers to both survive and return home but to Papee's relief both his sons did!

The family thought the weight of their prayers at home had made the difference. Stuart was awarded the Distinguished Flying Cross (DFC) and returned to Sydney, after a short squadron posting to New Guinea, at the end of the war. In 1945, Stuart finished his flying career as Squadron Leader.

With his Lancaster experience he had an opportunity to join the emerging commercial airline industry but Papee needed him at his law firm.

Stuart did his duty and completed his law degree and joined the family law firm of J Stuart Thom & Co. Jenny, still in love, followed Stuart to Australia hoping there would be a future there for her but once again Stuart did his duty and returned to his wife Mary. Without a future in Australia, Jenny returned home to England. Mary and the rest of the family in Australia, other than Norm and Margery, were not aware of her existence.

Stuart was known to often leave his office and drive to the airport at Mascot, sitting for hours in his car watching the aircraft land and take off. Stuart eventually found solace in yachting through their neighbour, who was building a yacht next door and joined the Royal Prince Alfred Yacht Club at Pittwater. Stuart enjoyed the teamwork in sailing that he had missed since being in command of a Lancaster and its crew. At the yacht club, he went on to be Officer of the Day for many years and didn't forget Molly's son, Ian who helped him crew the Officer of the Days' boat. Stuart was made a life member of RPAYC in 1982. At age 69, Stuart died from lung cancer. Norm cried for him at the funeral.

Clark Gable

Following America's entry into the war after the Japanese attack on Pearl Harbour, U.S. airmen started to arrive in England in the middle of 1942. They built new bases and operated separately from the RAF. The U.S. 8th Air Force bombed the enemy in daylight. They relied on tight defensive formations from their B17 Flying Fortresses and the firepower from twin 0.50 calibre machine guns in turrets in the nose, upper fuselage, belly and tail. With a service ceiling of between 25,000 ft and 35,000 ft they could be above the worst of the German anti-aircraft fire. By bombing in daylight, they boasted they would be able to do precision bombing. They would show the RAF how to do it!

Norm found the Americans very cocky and loud, but this was before their first combat mission. Before they had been tested.

The U.S. 8th Air Force flew their first mission on 17th August 1942 and the German fighters soon started taking a heavy toll on the B17's. Long range anti-aircraft guns capable of exploding flak at the height the B17s were flying were also rapidly deployed against them. By the summer of 1943, the B17 was armed with no less than 13 machine guns. It fairly bristled with machine guns and required a crew of 10. The German Luftwaffe in 1943 was at peak strength against the American bombers and found a weakness to the B17 defensive formation, attacking them from the front.

The pilots flying the ME-109's and FW-190's were experienced professionals. The best in the world! Some of the German pilots had been flying in combat since 1936. Many had dozens of aerial victories; some had over 100. This was a battle between professionals and amateurs. Both sides were incredibly brave but the American losses were terribly high. It was common for over 30 aircraft per mission to be lost. That was 300 men killed on one mission! In 1943, American bomber crews were tasked with a 25-mission tour of duty. Most crews never made it past their fifth.

The Luftwaffe owned the skies over Europe and the men of the 8th Air Force were paying the price. Norm liked the Americans and said of them, 'They talked big, but they died big.' Every time a B17 was shot down 10 aircrew died and the need for recruitment was high. They needed someone to put out the message.

In August 1942, the American film star, Clark Gable, enlisted in the Army and trained as an aerial gunner. He arrived in England in April 1943 and was promoted to Captain. His main purpose, according to the US Air Force, was to make recruitment movies and star in recruitment events but Clark Gable wanted to be just like the other aerial gunners he had trained with and fly in combat. He flew in five official missions, on one he was missed by a German cannon shell by an inch. He was very brave and unofficially, he flew in more missions but the authorities were trying to wrap him in cotton wool. They didn't want to lose him. Hitler had personally put a price on his head and his loss would have been a propaganda victory to the Germans and a big loss to the American recruiting campaign.

Clark Gable & Crew

On an occasion later in 1943, Norm visited the Cambridge Cemetery to do his duty and officiate at the funeral of an Australian airman. The British bury their dead with great reverence and Norm was satisfied that the airman's family would have been pleased with the service. Norm had been doing that duty for over six months and was finding it more depressing each time. Because of the increasing fatalities from

Training Command they started to bury them in crew lots and not individually. He was now tiring of death being his companion for over two years.

Norm decided he would go into London to have a few drinks and stay the night. He was in full dress uniform from the funeral and made his way to the Savoy Hotel. He was having a drink at the bar when the barman told him Clark Gable had put out an invitation for any airman who came in to join him for a drink in his suite. Norm found Gable to be very good company with a genuine interest in other airmen's experiences and a strong desire to be just one of the boys. He loved the comradeship of his fellow airmen, enjoyed his whisky, was always impeccably dressed and liked to wear cowboy boots. He was unable to go into the street for fear he would be mobbed, particularly by women. His movie 'Gone with the Wind' released just before the war had made him the most famous and desirable man in the world. Because of this, Clark Gable stayed in his suite in the Savoy but kept his door open to other airmen when he was there.

Norm caught up with Clark again in August. He asked Norm to bring his ambulance driver fiancée with him when next in London. One month later, Norm called in to Clark Gable's suite with Margery by his side, the noise of boisterous talking and laughter from about 10 American airmen died to a whisper as they appreciated a beautiful woman in uniform had entered their midst. They were very respectful. Norm and Margery stayed about 30 minutes and received genuine good wishes for their future from Clark and all his friends. Talking with Clark and his USAF friends, Norm got an appreciation for the American effort and the heavy losses they were suffering.

KETTLEBY THORPE FARM

On the 21st May 1943, Norm had an appointment at Buckingham Palace to be decorated with his DFM by the King. This was the third time he had met King George VI and the King recognised him again, possibly because of Norm's red hair and blue RAAF uniform. He said, 'Good to see you're still here, thank you for your service, I hope you get home safely, good luck.' Norm had taken his brother Stuart to the Palace and between them, over the next two days in London, they drank all the £20 pound bonus that came with the medal.

Norm & Stuart outside Buckingham Palace

It was a good time for Norm. He had recovered from his injuries and had the company of Stuart while he was at Norm's OTU. His romance with Margery was going well and he had been very proud to introduce her to Stuart.

It was now July 1943 and the middle of summer. The days were warm and long. The Lincolnshire countryside was beautiful, and Norm and Margery were able to enjoy some relaxing days touring the county and visiting local pubs like the Bluebell. They were in love and Margery felt it was time to introduce her Australian pilot to her family. The next day the forecast was for fine weather and the base had very little activity planned. Margery asked Group Captain Drane Lowe for the use of a vehicle so she could take Norm to see the farm and meet her family.

Drane, who was always happy to facilitate Norm and Margery's romance agreed. Margery told him they would fill the vehicle with diesel at the farm because being a working farm producing food for the people, they were allowed by the Government as much fuel as they needed. At this time the OTU was based at Saltby in Leicestershire and it would be an easy two-hour drive to Kettleby Thorpe farm in North Lincolnshire. From Saltby, with Margery driving, they passed through Grantham and then on to Lincoln where Norm showed her the road where he touched his Lancaster's wing tip on the bitumen. From Lincoln they passed through the lovely market town of Brigg and Margery pulled to the side of the road to show Norm the prisoner of war camp located on Pingley Farm on the outskirts of the town. There were about 1,500 prisoners there, mainly Italian and some German. Margery warned Norm he would see some POW's at work on the farm.

They and other farms in the area had an arrangement with the prison camp that every morning they would ring the local farmers and enquire as to how many workers they would need that day. Margery said in amusement that her father or brothers would always reply, 'Two Italians or one German in that proportion and we need 10 today.'

'Norm, we only have three miles to go and Kettleby is on the left,' said Margery as she drove on. Norm noticed it was beautiful farming country with crops ready for harvest.

Margery turned into an unmarked driveway. 'This is home, Norm.' Ahead was a long driveway leading to a very large two story, eight-bedroom house and to the right of the main house were substantial farm buildings in red brick and slate roofs, further on was another two story, four-bedroom house. In all it was a very impressive farm. In the fields Norm noticed about eight men picking up and loading hay on to large trailer being towed by a tractor. They looked different and Margery said they were Italian. Norm and Margery had both worn their uniforms and Norm, who wanted to see the enemy close up wondered if they would be intimidated by their uniforms. Margery said the Italians wouldn't be because they were happy to see out the war on the farm. They were well treated there and enjoyed the farm work. She was not sure of the Germans reaction but said there was nothing to worry about.

There was a welcoming committee for them at the main farmhouse. Norm first met Margery's father, James Morwood, a tall, straight figure who was wearing a tweed coat and tie and long boots. James then introduced his wife and Margery's mother and then Margery's three sisters who were giggling in their excitement. Margery's two brothers were still in the fields supervising the POW labour from the prison camp.

Kettleby Thorpe farm covered 300 acres on the Bigby High road. James Morwood ran his farm with the help of his two sons, John and Rowland. Margery also had three sisters, Edith, Florence and Gladys. They were all excited to meet Margery's beau. Norm was the first Australian they met. It had been all the talk the past week that Margery was bringing Norman, the Australian Bomber pilot that she had fallen in love with, to home. Until the war, their community rarely travelled and knew little of the outside world. Now everything had changed. As Lincolnshire was flat and suitable for landing fields most of Bomber Command were based there, along with thousands of airmen, ground staff and support staff from many foreign countries like Australia, Canada, New Zealand, America and Africa. The culture of their country had changed in a short time.

Margery's sisters had gathered around her and were hugging and laughing and asking so many questions and Norm was talking to her parents. Margery's brothers, John and Rowland having seen the Air Force vehicle coming up the drive, appeared from the fields on their tractors. They introduced themselves to Norm. They were both big, strong men with big hands from a lifetime of farm work. Norm noticed their strong North Lincolnshire accents and thought it strange that he had not noticed a strong accent with Margery.

John said to Margery, 'Aye lass, thou are here at last. Dost tha mind if we talk to Norman?' John and Rowland led Norm away and asked him questions about Australia and Bomber Command and his opinion of the war situation. All the time Norm knew that they were feeling him out for their sister Margery. They laughed at some of Norm's stories. He was a good storyteller. Rowland told Norm of a fright they had about three months before. It was about 1am and the sirens went off and German planes flew right over the farm. Rowland called out that gas was coming in the windows. They all put their gas masks on and sat on the stairs for over an hour. Then their father went outside to check the stock and all the cows were chewing their cud and the horses were okay. He took off his mask and realised it was just fog. After that night they got used to German planes flying over and it did not worry them.

John was very close to Margery. When he left school at 14 he worked the farm as the 'Wagoner' from dawn to dark and Margery, who was then eight years old, would go with him to supper up the horses at night. Margery would carry the lantern for John while he worked through the stables. She did this every night for years and the bond and love formed between them would last forever.

Margery's family at Kettleby Thorpe farm

Norm asked the brothers if he would be able to see the POW's. John said, 'Aye Norman but father will not allow the lasses near the Italians. They are terrible flirts. Come and sit thee on the back of the tractor.' John then drove back to the field with Norm on the back and stopped next to the workers. They were remarkably friendly and happy at their work. They called out, 'Salve, da dove viene quell' uniforme.' (Hello, where is that uniform from?) Norm worked the translation out and called back, 'Australia.' That caused excitement among the POW's. 'After the war we all come to Australia,' they called. Norm gave them a laugh and a big thumbs up. When the war finished the Italians returned home straight away but for the German POW's returning home was a complicated affair. If their home in Germany was now under the control of the Russian communists, they did not want to go home and the

Pingley Prison Farm looked after them till 1948 when many of them settled in England.

Norm returned to his airbase in very high spirits and reported to Drane Lowe that the meeting with Margery's family had gone well and he loved the farm. Norm was excited and Drane was pleased. Norm had changed from the edgy, aggressive young man who had come to him from 97 Squadron and was now more mellow and believing he may have a future. Margery had changed him.

As Norm wrote about the Morwood family in his notes, *'Her parents, her brothers and sisters were all terrific people and I am pleased to say that my marriage was a very, very good idea.'*

'Well Norm,' Drane said, 'are you going to ask her to marry you?'

'Not yet,' said Norm. 'My home is Australia. If I survive the war and return home, would she leave her family behind and travel to the other side of the world to be with me?'

Drane replied, 'If you are both in love and want to marry then do so, the war is not over! Have your happiness while you are young and alive. If you survive the war think about the future then.'

Norm thought for a minute and said, 'Thanks Drane, I'll think about it.'

'You know Norm, you and Margery are both friends of mine and in my OTU we never get any good news around here. As you know too well it's been all death and injuries and funerals for years. If you and Margery did decide to get married it would be a change and a morale boost to the whole OTU. Here is a couple planning a future together in the middle of the war!'

Norm thought for a minute again, 'Okay Drane, I'll ask her.'

When Norm took trainees up in his Wellington, he now made a habit to fly over Kettleby Thorpe Farm, waggle his aircraft's wings and throw the shadow of the aircraft over the farmhouse. That way they knew it was him flying the aircraft and saying hello. One day he did that and noticed that Rowland was in the fields on his tractor. He did another circuit and came down very low to about 15 ft off the ground heading straight at Rowland. Rowland had observed the bomber flying over the farm and guessed it was Norm now heading straight for him and assumed he would pull up so was not overly concerned but the bomber kept coming at about 200 miles an hour. Rowland jumped off the tractor and the Wellington thundered over the top barely missing by 10 ft. Rowland would later say it was only three inches!

Norm still loved low flying and his continued disdain and lack of respect for military discipline combined one day to make him do something that would risk his whole Air Force career. He was in the air one fine summer's day with a bunch of trainees. He heard that a nearby airbase was having a large ceremonial parade for an Air Commodore. Norm, who had been in high spirits recently because of his success in courting Margery could not help himself and headed for the airbase to have a look. From 5,000 ft he looked down and could see a large group of airmen and women lined up neatly, parading in front of the Air Commodore. For Norm this was too much!

He took the Wellington on a wide circuit of the airbase, reduced his altitude to about 50 ft and at full speed of 230 mph beat up the parade. It all happened so quickly that no one was able to get the Wellingtons number. The Air Commodore was furious and took the beat up of his parade as a personal attack and vowed to get the culprit and either hang him or kick him out of the Force. Norm returned to his base and told Drane Lowe what he had done. Drane swore at him and told him he would be on toilet duties for a month. Then he said, 'Leave it with me, Norm.'

Drane organised Norm's crew of trainees to depart the base for a couple of days and keep their silence. They had enjoyed the beat up as much as Norm! The Wellington went straight to the hanger and was stripped down so it looked like it hadn't flown for days. The Military Police, looking for the offending Wellington, had about six airbases to search where it could have come from. When they arrived at Norm's OTU some hours later, Group Captain Lowe told them the offending Wellington was not from his base and showed them the stripped-down Wellington in the hanger. It was the only aircraft on the base and now in pieces and could not possibly have been flying two hours earlier! As nobody had recorded the aircraft's number correctly during the beat up, the search for the culprit failed. Norm was lucky again. Drane had got him off the hook.

With Margery on his mind Norm went to see her in the sick bay. He wanted to plan an afternoon together the next day, the 1st August, his birthday. This, he hoped would give him an opportunity and a better chance of a favourable reply when he popped the question. Margery was pleased and said she would organise a nice picnic for his birthday.

James Morwood (Margery's father) standing by the brook and shady trees where Norm proposed to Margery

It was summer and the days were very long. It didn't get dark till 10pm. He would have plenty of time to find the courage in these beautiful long and lazy summer days. They arranged to have the picnic at the farm. Behind the farmhouse ran a brook surrounded by shady trees and Margery had brought a blanket and a picnic that her sisters had helped prepare. It was here, on a warm sunny day in the shade of the trees with the brook babbling away at their feet, that Norm asked Margery to marry him. Margery didn't hesitate and said, 'Yes, of course Norm.'

Now they were engaged and with Drane's advice in mind, Norm wanted the wedding to happen soon and Margery agreed, suggesting a three-month engagement would give them time to organise all the things a bride needs to do. Together they set the wedding date for early November. Margery told her family and there was much excitement. 'Will you be going to Australia?' they wanted to know.

'If we survive the war I will think about it then but if Norm wants to return to Australia then I will go with him.'

Drane was delighted when Norm told him and put the happy news on the notice board so the whole of 14 OTU could share in the news that two of their colleagues were planning a future together and getting married.

It was August 1943 and though losses were still horrific there were signs the tide of war was changing. The Germans had been defeated at Stalingrad in February and Bomber Command, along with the U.S. 8th Air Force were inflicting increasing damage on German cities. The war was now at its peak and any tiny bit of good news was welcomed as relief from the bad news of war.

On the 6th November 1943, at Bigby Parish Church situated next door to Margery's farm, Norm and Margery were married.

Stuart was the best man and many from Norm and Margery's OTU attended the happy occasion. Photos and the reception were at Kettleby Thorpe Farm.

Norm and Margery's wedding photo

They went to London for their honeymoon and stayed at the Savoy Hotel. Clark Gable had just left and returned to America.

After a short honeymoon, Norm and Margery returned to the cottage they had leased at 18 Hillside Avenue, Kettering. Many parties were held there. Stuart had commenced his operational tour with 463 squadron and he and Jenny were regular visitors. They were very happy times for them all. Margery fell pregnant and left the WAAF on compassionate grounds in March 1944. On the 9th August 1944, they had a baby son, James Stuart Lindsay Crouch.

As the year drew to a close, it was obvious the war in Europe was turning in the Allies favour. The D-Day invasion of Normandy on the 6th June had been successful and the Germans were retreating on two fronts. Bomber Command and the U.S. 8th Air Force were inflicting enormous damage on German cities and their military infrastructure. Norm, Margery and their friends were starting to see the chance of victory and the end of the war. It was time to look to the future.

Meanwhile in Sydney, Papee was fuming that his son had not yet received a commission. He wrote a 'dirty' letter to the Australian Government in Canberra demanding they rectify this with the RAF. As a result Norm was promoted from Warrant Officer to Flight Lieutenant in a matter of months. Norm was not really happy because he had enjoyed his Warrant Officer rank.

The end of the war in Europe came with the German surrender on 8th May 1945. Norm and Margery, along with Drane Lowe and some friends from his OTU, went to London to join the VE Day parades and celebrations. The war was over and the streets were full of people. They were all singing and laughing and the girls were kissing all the men in uniform including Norm and Drane. Margery said, 'Let's go to the palace and see the King.' A crowd had already gathered there. There must have been fifty thousand people around Buckingham Palace all calling for the King.

King George VI, who had shared so much of the sufferings of his people, even having his own home bombed and not running away to the country during the 'Blitz' or later when the V-bombs were raining down on London, appeared on the balcony dressed in naval uniform and accompanied by the Queen. Happy and smiling, he waved to the crowd below. They cheered him and sang the National Anthem.

'Where's Winnie?' someone called and the chant went up, 'We want Winston, we want Winston.' The King spread out his arms to indicate Winston Churchill was not there. The crowd started singing, 'For He's a Jolly Good Fellow,' and after that the King waved and left the balcony.

Norm, Margery and Drane started heading to Whitehall with some of the crowd looking for Churchill. Outside the Ministry of Health building a Salvation Army Band were playing 'Land of Hope and Glory' and Winston appeared on the balcony to enormous applause. He lit his cigar to more applause from the crowd and started to conduct the band with his lit cigar to 'Onward Christian Soldiers' and the crowd joined in. It was a wonderful day and a fitting climax.

'Well Norm that's it; it's all over! I expect to get orders to shut down the Unit in the next few days,' said Drane.

Norm never showed physical emotion or affection in the past but now, with the emotion all around them and the heady feeling of victory, he placed a hand on Drane's shoulder and said, 'Thank you, Drane. It was good being with you the last two years, we did make a difference, didn't we?'

Drane put his hand on Norm's shoulder and said, 'Yes Norm, we made a big difference, lost so many friends and in the end, we were lucky and survived. We will have to lead good lives to repay that luck.'

Drane told Norm he could get him a permanent commission in the RAF as an experimental Hunter pilot but thought he would not like it much. Norm agreed.

'Thanks very much, Drane but Margery and Jimmy and me will go home to Australia. It's such a big country that there should be a good future there as a pilot in the airline industry.'

'That sounds like a good plan, good luck Norm,' said Drane, who then gave Margery a farewell kiss and turned around and disappeared into the crowd.

RETURN TO AN UNGRATEFUL COUNTRY

Norm and Margery planned for their future in Australia. They left their lovely cottage in Kettering where they had lived happily for almost two years during the war. Margery and Jimmy returned to live at Kettleby Thorpe Farm. Norm departed from the U.K. on 28th June 1945 and arrived in Sydney via the Panama Canal on the 28th July 1945.

Family photo – beach Australia

There was no welcome.

All the interest in Australia was about the Japanese war. The few remaining survivors returning from Bomber

Command in Europe had fought the enemy well before the Japanese involvement had seen many of their friends killed in the deadliest theatre of World War II, flying in freezing and terrifying conditions. They were ignored and forgotten. There was even criticism of their part in the total warfare and the destruction of German cities with their civilian population.

As Norm would say, 'That was the war that was, and we were forced into it by the Nazi's. Coming second in total warfare with the Nazis doesn't bear thinking about.'

All Norm received on his return was 200 pounds back-pay and a pinstriped suit to look smart while applying for a job. The only work he was offered was that of a grave digger. How inappropriate! He found himself on the job scrapheap.

Meanwhile Margery and Jimmy said goodbye to their family in England and in December 1945 boarded the MS Rangatiki at Tilbury Docks with many other war brides and sailed via the Suez Canal, arriving in Australia in January 1946.

CIVIL FLYING CAREER

Norm took lessons in Morse Code to increase his chances of getting a job as a pilot with one of the civilian airlines that were starting up. In his own words:

'As soon as I could, I applied for a flying job with Australian National Airway (ANA) and TAA which was just being formed. I got the job with ANA but they had too many pilots so I was sacked before I started. However, TAA came good and I joined on 12th August 1946. It was a very funny airline to start with. Three groups fought for power in the first two years: The East Sale mob, Guinea Airways, and Qantas. East Sale won and controlled the airline for many years.

Promotion to Captain was due to who you knew and not what you knew. A few Guinea Airways pilots were First Officers with Guinea and promoted immediately to Captain. One particular pilot had never flown at night and could not fly instruments at all. His first night flight was flown by a RAF trained Flight Officer. That Captain was eventually persuaded to resign.

There were others equally as bad. I started as a Flight Officer mainly because in the RAF, flying hours only were recorded. In the RAAF, flying and taxiing hours were counted and this doubled your logbook hours. Also unfortunately, some pilots faked their logbook hours. Anyway, I had some three years as an F/O on DC3's and DC4's. During this time I went on loan to

British Commonwealth Pacific Airlines, the oddest airline ever to fly. My first trip with them was an uneventful one to Honolulu. However, from Honolulu to Los Angeles the Captain was blind drunk so I took off and landed in Los Angeles. Little did he know it was my first take-off and landing in the left seat of a DC4.

Many equally bizarre things happened in the next few years and the airline was amalgamated with Qantas after a crash which killed everyone. While as an F/O, we were busy building a house in Turramurra. With it just finished, I was posted to Brisbane as a Captain. It was the best thing as we bought an old house at Shornecliffe. The house was big and beautiful and we were very happy. The five-day western was all the rage. Five days flying all over Queensland and in summer it was an incredibly hard slog with very few navigation aids and continuous turbulence.'

The family had now grown with the arrival of two daughters, Rosemary and Carolyn. They all knew when Norm was coming home because he would fly over the house and waggle his wings and throw the aircraft's shadow over the house. The same thing he used to do over Kettleby Thorpe farm in England.

'To further my career, I took a posting to Melbourne to fly DC3's, DC4's and Viscount aircraft. During this time, I became active in the Pilots Federation and served for two years as the Victorian Branch Chairman. I had a short time on Electra aircraft, then in 1966 I went to San Diego and did the

jet course on Boeing 727's with Pacific Southwest Airlines (PSA). This was the best course ever.

I stayed at the Bahia Motel, worked like hell and loved San Diego. Came back to Melbourne and flew the 727's, except for two years on DC9's, for the rest of my flying career. The 727 was a great aircraft and many of the trips, particularly to Perth and the three-day trip to Darwin were greatly enjoyed.

During my career I was asked to transfer to The Flying Tigers, Varig in Brazil, British Commonwealth Pacific Airlines (BCPA) and to stay in San Diego with Pacific South-west Airlines (PSA). However, Australia won out and on reflection, I did the wise thing.'

In Melbourne, the family had settled in the leafy suburb of Eltham at 14 Park road. In June 1957, in the early hours of the morning, the family were awakened by a loud crackling and popping noise and rushed from bed into the corridor to see the laundry was well alight and the fire already in the ceiling.

James (Jimmy) recalled, 'There was no time to fight it or recover anything and all we could do was make sure everybody got out. We all ended up outside, standing on the road in our pyjamas, watching our house burn down. It appeared the kerosene heater in the laundry had caught fire and as it was a weatherboard house it burned fiercely and within an hour despite the arrival of the fire brigade was just smoking rubble.'

Norm and Margery lost everything, but everyone survived or so the family thought. Norm's mother, Mabel was visiting from Sydney and was nowhere to be found. Everyone searched franticly and most of the neighbours rallied around. One of them said Mabel had gone into the house across the road. Margery went and checked and Nanna (Mabel) was safe there, having a cup of tea. The author, Alan Marshall who lived there with his sister, Elsie McConnel had come and taken Nanna inside when the rest of the family were distracted by the fire.

James said, 'Kind neighbours took us in for the night and we were able to find emergency accommodation for a few days until we found a rental property.'

Norm and Margery lost all their personal belongings. Searching through the ashes the next day, Jimmy found all Norm's war medals. They were all that could be recovered. A reporter took a photo of him recovering the medals and it appeared in the Herald Sun next day. It was a tragedy that both Norm and Margery had lost their personal records from the war. However, they both wrote their memoirs in later years as well as they could remember them.

Jimmy – newspaper photo with medals

Three years later, Norm and Margery had another son, Philip Norman.

Remembering his over four years' service in Bomber Command, the tears for the losses in this bitter struggle against Germany and the lack of appreciation or assistance to those few survivors who returned home, Norm described politicians as 'urgers'; those who would urge others to do the working, the fighting and the dying. He resolved that the most pompous of them would get some humility.

It was a Monday morning at Essendon Airport in Melbourne and Norm was Captain of a turbo prop Lockheed Electra flight to Canberra. Many politicians were returning to Canberra after a weekend at home. It was departure time and he hadn't had clearance from the ground engineer below him to start his engines. Norm opened his cockpit window stuck his head out and yelled, 'What are we waiting for, Tom?'

Tom, the ground engineer called back, 'I've been told to hold for a VIP.'

'What bloody VIP?' yelled Norm.

The ground engineer, who was a friend of Norms yelled back, 'Pull your head back in, Norm or I'll get the egg board to stamp it,' in reference to the fact that Norm was balding. 'It's a politician,' Tom called.

'Bloody hell,' yelled Norm and slammed his window closed. Two minutes later the Federal politician, Billie Mackie Snedden walked across the tarmac in full view of the passengers on the aircraft who were wondering why their flight was delayed. He could have run to save time but would not have looked important doing that. The flight departed four minutes late and when the aircraft reached cruising altitude, Norm instructed the senior hostess to invite Mr Snedden to meet the Captain in the cockpit. 'Good day Sir,' said Norm. 'Why did you, as a servant of the public, keep my passengers waiting?'

Norm was to ask that question of many politicians over the years and once asked it of the President of the Australian Council of Trade Unions who would later become a Prime Minister. Mr Hawke would later disparage airline pilots as being 'glorified bus drivers' and then have his revenge during the pilots dispute. On two occasions, miffed politicians reported Norm to Sir Robert Law-Smith, a Commissioner of TAA and a director of Qantas. Sir Robert however, being fully aware of Norm's war record and having himself been a Squadron Leader in the RAAF from 1940 to 1946, empathised with Norm and gave him a token 'slap on the wrist'.

Norm had an unsettling experience while landing his Boeing 727 at Coolangatta Airport in a rainstorm when the aircraft aquaplaned down the runway only just coming to a stop at the end of the runway, even after full reverse thrust was applied to its mighty jet engines. Norm had a flashback to 35 years before, returning from that first mission in the Lancaster where they scraped to a halt on their belly, only just avoiding going over the edge of a quarry at the end of the field.

Finally feeling his nerves were shot after that incident, Norm retired in 1977 with over 23,000 flying hours in his logbook.

The Crouch family in Australia

Victorian Branch Chairman.

Had a short time on Electra aircraft then in 1966 I went to San Diego and did the jet course course on Boeing 727's with Pacific South West Airlines (P.S.A) this course was the best ever. Stayed at the BAHIA Motel worked like hell and loved San Diego.

Came back to Melbourne and flew the 727's (except for 2 years on DC9's) for the rest of my flying career. The 727 was a great aircraft and many of the trips particularly to Perth and the 3 day trips to Darwin were greatly enjoyed.

Finished in July 1977 with over 23 000 hours in my log book. It, for the most part, was a grand life. CRy nerves were not too good when I called it a day and I was content to retire.

During my career I was asked to transfer to the Flying Tigers, Varig in Brazil, BCPA and also to stay in San Diego with PSA However Australia won out and in reflection I probably did the wise thing.

① which made me the first Australian to fly Lancasters.

② During this time I became official mourner for 92 group and every Tuesday I went to the Oxford Cemetery and supervised the funerals of any Australian killed. The English bury their dead with great reverence. As a reward I had one night in London on the return trip.

③ During the whole of my air force career I was crazy about low flying and could flying quite easily at 2-3 feet above the ground. While on the Squadron we had times when the maximum hight allowed was 100'. I got caught in Lincoln one day when my bottom wing was way below the buildings and a policeman on duty took the makers number which was about the size of a car number plate. However it was

Norm's handwritten notes - Retirement

RETIREMENT

ater in 1977, Norm and Margery bought 22 acres of land in Doreen just 10 minutes from the Greensborough family home. The intention was to breed Angora goats and keep themselves busy in their retirement. They built a house and sheds and Norm built a lot of fencing; the hard, physical labour was not something he was used to. His previous idea of physical labour was 18 holes of golf. Norm was always a keen golfer, playing pennant golf off a single figure handicap for his Club, the Heidelberg Golf Club.

Norm and Margery enjoyed running their Angora stud and having their children and grandchildren visit and help with the young goats. Margery, being a farmer's daughter, enjoyed it the most. After about four years, the bottom fell out of the Angora market. It turned out to be just another fad.

They were getting older and Norm wanted to concentrate more on his golf so they moved back to their house in Greensborough and sold the farm to James and Margaret.

Norm spent his time between home, the Greensborough RSL and the Heidelberg Golf Club.

In 1982, Norm travelled to Toronto, Canada to catch up with his two Canadian gunners, Bill Townley and Jack Oates. Bill had organised the reunion at his house in Toronto. It was a great reunion and they enjoyed their reminiscences as only those who had been a Bomber Command team would understand. A guest at the reunion had rudely criticised the civilian casualties in Germany which annoyed them all, coming from someone who had spent the war in Canada never under the threat of attack or seeing the consequences of war.

From Canada, Norm flew on to England to visit Margery's family and to catch up with some friends from the war. It was not very successful and Norm commented on his return to Australia that 40 years of peace had changed them; they were not the same people he had remembered.

Back home in Melbourne, Norm and Margery were content in their retirement for many years until, in 1995, Norm climbed a tree with a bush saw in hand to prune it. He fell out of the tree and damaged his knee which put an end to his golf.

In 2001, he was diagnosed with bowel cancer. He continued marching with the Greensborough RSL on ANZAC Day and in his last year, 2003, was assisted with a wheelchair. The cancer had spread to his liver.

Norm passed away at home in the care of his family on 8th July 2003.

This book was written to tell Norm's story and to address the poor welcome home that the few surviving Bomber Command aircrew received.

It seemed for the Australian authorities to remember and laud these men's courage, raised a difficult moral issue about the bombing of the civilian population in German cities. The Australian Government didn't do anything and our airmen were denied the honour and respect due to them. In contrast, the enemy and aggressor, Nazi Germany, boasted of their success in destroying the English city of Coventry using the word 'coventried' to describe further successes in destroying English targets and their civilian populations.

The Allies knew it was unthinkable to lose to Nazi Germany. The atrocities revealed after the war confirmed that. It was total warfare and pursued relentlessly by Bomber Command.

Norm was very lucky. His war was an adventure.

EPILOGUE

The shock of Norm's cancer pushed Margery into dementia and the family cared for her at the same time. The family built a granny flat on the farm and she was cared for there by her family and professional carers. She was very strong and grateful and full of grace.

Margery lived until the 28th August 2016. She was 96 years old.

Even though Margery had lived in Australia for 70 years she was an Englishwoman and in her purse kept Hymn 655 Jerusalem. This was Margery:

> *'And did those feet in ancient time*
> *Walk upon England's mountains green?*
> *And was the holy lamb of God*
> *On England's pleasant pastures seen?*
> *And did the countenance divine*
> *Shine forth upon our clouded hills?*
> *And was Jerusalem builded here*
> *Among these dark satanic mills?*
> *Bring me my bow of burning gold!*
> *Bring me my arrows of desire!*
> *Bring me my spear, oh clouds unfold!*
> *Bring me my chariot of fire!*
> *I will not cease from mental fight,*

Nor shall my sword sleep in my hand

Till we have built Jerusalem

In England's green and pleasant land.

For those caring for a loved one with dementia Margery would like you to know:

Do not ask me to remember,

Don't try to make me understand,

Let me rest and know you're with me,

Kiss my cheek and hold my hand.

I'm confused beyond your concept,

I am sad and sick and lost.

All I know is that I need you

To be with me at all cost.

Do not lose patience with me,

Do not scold or curse or cry.

I can't help the way I'm acting,

Can't be different though I try.

Just remember that I need you

That the best of me is gone,

Please don't fail to stand beside me,

Love me 'til my life is done.

(Author unknown)

My parents, Francis Norman 'Norm' Crouch and Margery Crouch

BIBLIOGRAPHY

Press, Nigel, '*Into Thin Air*': *The Story of a Bomber Station at War. RAF Woodhall Spa 1941-1945T*

    Tucann Design & Print.

Bending, Kevin, '*Achieve Your Aim*'. The History of 97 (Straights Settlements) Squadron in the Second World War.

    Woodfield Publishing.

Brickhill, Paul, '*The Dam Busters*'

    Pan Books.

Currie, Jack DFC. '*The Augsburg Raid*'

    Goodall Publications Ltd

McCarthy, John. *Martin, Sir Harold Brownlow (Mick). Australian Dictionary of Biography*

The Blitz

    www.primaryhomeworkhelp.co.uk/war/blitz.htm

Clark Gable

    Stanchak, John E. *Captain Hollywood*

    https://en.m.wikipedia.org/wiki/Clark.Gable

The Convoy

    www.warsailors.com/convoys/hx134report.html

Coventry

Coventry City Council-20 facts you might not know about the Coventry Blitz

Trueman, C.N. '*The bombing of Coventry in 1940*'

Coventry Blitz

https://en.m.wikipedia.org/wiki/Coventry-blitz

Empire Air Training Scheme

www.awm.gov.au/units/unit_14939.asp

http://home.st.net.au/~dunn/raaf/eats.htp

Kassell

https://en.m.wikipedia.org/wiki/Bombing_of_kassell_in_World_War_11

Pingley POW Camp- Brigg

Nigel Fisher's Brigg Blog

RAF Bomber Command

https://en.m.wikipedia.org/wiki/RAF_Bomber_Command#Organisation

TSS Awatea

www.offshore-radio.de/fleet/awatea.htm

US 8th Airforce

https://www.nationalww2museum.org/war/articles/eighth-air-force-vs-luftwaffe

ACKNOWLEDGMENTS

My father, Francis Norman Crouch, for his writings and stories.

My mother, Margery Crouch (Morwood), for her writings and stories.

Ian Webster, Past-Secretary of the Greensborough RSL, who became a friend of Norm's, and after his death in 2003 presented the family with a large folder detailing Norm's RAAF/RAF career.

Squadron Leader Stanley Harrison was Norm's skipper for his first 12 missions and presented him with his book 'A Bomber Command Survivor' from which I drew heavily.

Ian Hough, for the information on his parents; Lieutenant Reginald William Hough (Bill) and Mollicent Hough, and of his uncle, Stuart Crouch.

David Morwood, for information on Kettleby Thorpe Farm.

Rod Drakes, for information on Kettleby Thorpe Farm.

My sisters, Rosemary Valadon and Carolyn Morwood, and my brother, Phillip Crouch, for their help and encouragement.

My wife, Margaret Crouch, for her ongoing love and support.

The Publishers, Footprints Publishing. In particular, Claudette Pope for her professionalism, support and encouragement and Lisa Wolstenholme for her brilliant cover design.

Norm marching on ANZAC Day, Greensborough 2002.
"Doing it hard but determined to make it."

Norm 2003. His final ANZAC Day.
In a wheelchair pushed by Grandson "David."
Followed by Margery being helped by
Granddaughter "Alison."

Lightning Source UK Ltd.
Milton Keynes UK
UKHW022321310720
367511UK00006B/87

9 780648 714521